DIGITAL ASSETS AND PROBATE

A PRACTITIONER'S GUIDE

DIGITAL ASSETS AND PROBATE

A PRACTITIONER'S GUIDE

James Normington

Wildy, Simmonds and Hill Publishing

ISBN: 9780854902958

British Library Cataloguing in Publication Data

A catalogue record for this book is available from the British Library

First published in 2023 by

Wildy, Simmonds & Hill Publishing
Wildy & Sons Ltd
Lincoln's Inn Archway
Carey Street
London WC2A 2JD
www.wildy.com

Typeset by Heather Jones, North Petherton, Somerset.
Printed in Great Britain by CPI Group (UK) Ltd, Croydon CR0 4YY.

For Caitlin, Olivia and Joshua
Your love and support continue to bring out the best in me

Contents

Table of Cases

Table of Statutes

Table of Statutory Instruments

Table of European Legislation

Table of HM Revenue & Customs Manuals

Introduction

The legal system in England and Wales and the concepts of probate have evolved throughout the centuries, yet the underlying concepts and principles would still be familiar to Charles Dickens, Mr Jaggers[1] and the eighteenth-century jurist, Sir William Blackstone.[2] The trust and equity concepts and division of assets between beneficiaries have evolved down the centuries and now we have witnessed a sea change in the assets themselves. The Haversham estate of Dickens' *Great Expectations* required the sale of a brewery, several houses and a substantial number of stocks, bonds and monetary instruments. As we progress through the twenty-first century an estate may not contain any real assets, and we are approaching a time when all parts of the probate process may be dealt with electronically, including the client interactions, the filing of court documents, the grant of probate and the distributions. As reported by the BBC, during the COVID-19 pandemic we saw a dramatic increase in the use of video conferencing technology in courts of over 500% compared to the previous 12 months. Even contentious probate applications and trials have been dealt with remotely in relation to the hearing of evidence and submissions.[3]

For the most part, and to a greater or lesser extent, estates throughout the nineteenth and twentieth centuries mirrored the contents of the Haversham estate. Mr Jaggers and his hard-working clerk, Mr Wemmick, would have had little issue dealing with an estate in the mid-twentieth century as it was largely similar to an estate in the mid-nineteenth century. The assets may have increased in value over time, but the basics remained the same. It was still a case of dealing with real property such as houses, stocks, bonds, shares, bank accounts and the deceased's business affairs, as well as the important matters of dealing with the deceased's final wishes. In the twenty-first century, the expansion of our individual lives into the digital space has led to each of us creating a digital footprint. Arguably, for some the footprint is small, but for some clients it verges on a Yeti- or Sasquatch-sized digital footprint. That digital footprint has in most cases expanded to include assets or quasi-assets that poor old Jaggers could only

---

1 Charles Dickens, *Great Expectations* (1861).

2 Blackstone was a barrister, jurist and judge. He was called by Middle Temple and authored numerous legal works, including the *Commentaries on the Laws of England* (Clarendon Press, 1765), which was one of the best sellers of its day.

3 'Remote hearings for family courts "horribly cruel"', BBC News, 4 June 2020, www.bbc.co.uk/news.

have read about in the science fiction of HG Wells. In order to continue in that grand tradition of providing high quality client care, it is imperative for the twenty-first century probate practitioner to understand the extent to which our digital footprint has evolved and how that impacts the avenues and approaches probate practitioners utilise on a day-to-day basis. Gordon Moore's observation in 1965 that 'Change has never been this fast, and will never be this slow again', feels particularly apt for the 2020s.[4]

Throughout the course of this book, we look at each of the more common elements of our digital life; the challenges and pitfalls that each element raises; and the most appropriate avenue to deal with each element. In some cases, depending upon the particular digital element, there may be work that should be done with the lay client prior to death. In other cases, there are appropriate solutions that can be utilised by executors following the grant of probate. In some cases, there will be items of financial value to be distributed, and in other cases there may be nothing more than items of sentimental value. There will also be cases where the digital footprint at first blush appears to pass the test of an asset, only to fail it due to an inherent defect in the digital holding. Irrespective of which category we as probate practitioners encounter, it is important to understand the appropriate approach. By dividing this work into short, well-structured chapters, the aim is to allow the practitioner to dip into the work on an as-needed basis.

---

4 Gordon Moore was the co-founder of Intel computers. He made that comment in 1965 when computer processing power was increasing at a rapid rate.

Part 1
Glossary

Glossary

Blockchain — A shared, immutable ledger that facilitates the process of recording transactions and tracking assets in a business network. The blockchain acts like a conveyor belt, recording transactions as data linked to the preceding block of data. This continual linking of data provides an element of security against unauthorised changes as one cannot change one transaction on the blockchain without impacting the succeeding blocks of data. The asset which is recorded on the blockchain may be a tangible asset (such as a house, a car, cash or land) or intangible assets (such as intellectual property, patents, copyrights or branding) or a record of obligations, warranties and rights (such as a smart contract).

Blog — A regularly updated web page or website which is written in a conversational style and is usually maintained by an individual (known as the blogger) or a small group of individuals. The style and format are very similar to that of a newspaper's editorial page.

Cloud (including cloud accounts, cloud storage, etc) — A non-localised storage device that can be accessed through networked computing facilities. This non-localised drive provides remote data storage and processing services via the internet. One of the advantages of this non-localised drive is that the data can be recovered from any web-enabled location.

Crypto-currency — A digital record in which transactions are verified and records maintained by a decentralised system of networked computers using cryptography, rather than by a centralised banking system or traditional banking authority. A crypto-currency utilises individual crypto-tokens to facilitate trades and exchanges.

Cryptography — The technique of using codes to secure data for transmission from one place to another. The data is translated into a secure message using a cypher which is then coded and transmitted. It is then uncoded using a cypher key upon receipt by the receiving computer or device. This technique has been used for centuries to create and send secret messages. In the digital world it is used in a multitude of programmes and applications.

Crypto-token — A cryptographic asset which exists on a blockchain. This type of cryptographic coin or token shares common identifying features with other similar coins or tokens. While it may have a unique access code or identifying markers, it is materially no different from any other coin or token in its class. It may be sold and exchanged and is fungible in nature, which means it is distinct from non-fungible tokens. There are unique tax and accounting rules which apply to transactions and exchanges involving crypto-tokens.

Digital asset — A digital record that can be stored and transmitted electronically through a computer or other digital device such as a mobile phone and has associated ownership or user rights. Examples of digital assets include digital photographs, crypto-currencies and non-fungible tokens.

Digital executor — An individual appointed under a last will and testament to perform the personal representative's and/or executor's duties in relation to an individual's digital assets and digital estate. The digital executor follows the wishes of the individual and distributes the assets to the beneficiaries by providing them with the necessary information. Furthermore, a digital executor may be instructed to copy, distribute or delete files as well as manage social media profiles and post messages on various sites and platforms.

Digital management — The process of storing, organising, managing and retrieving digital files including digital assets. Digital management may include copying, distributing or deleting files as well as managing digital content and social media profiles, including posting messages on various sites and platforms.

This may include documents such as ebooks, digital video, photography and sound recordings.

Digital pathways The actual access points which individuals use to access their digital world. This is more than just 'the internet' and specifically means the method or ways in which individuals establish their digital footprint. This could be by using particular applications, or particular hardware such as via a desktop PC, a laptop computer or a mobile phone.

Digital wallet A form for storing or holding crypto-tokens in one place. These digital wallets may exist in a physical form that can be removed from the computer hardware, similar to a flash drive or a removeable memory stick. The advantage of the physical form is that it can be completely removed from the worldwide web. This means that these physical types of digital wallets can be securely stored in a safe or other physical location. They can also exist in a digital application-based format, which can be accessed remotely using an internet connection. This makes the digital application version very accessible and does not require transportation of the physical drive or stick.

Ecommerce The process of buying and selling of goods and/or services using an internet-enabled computing device such as a tablet computer, a desktop PC or a smartphone.

Fungible An item that is easy to exchange for the same item of like value. For example, one share in a public limited company which trades on the London Stock Exchange is a fungible asset because it can be swapped for any other single share in that same company as both shares are exactly the same and have the same market price.

Hardware The physical components of a computer or computing system. These can be designed to be removeable in the form of a portable memory such as a flash drive or memory card. Alternatively, hardware can be non-portable, permanent physical components of the computing system such as a keyboard, a central processing unit (CPU), speakers or a motherboard.

HTML	Hypertext Markup Language. A markup language for the web. It defines the structure of web pages, incorporating text, graphics, sound, video and hyperlinks.
Non-fungible	An item that is unique in form and therefore not easy to exchange for the same item of like value or like type. For example, Thomas Gainsborough's painting, *The Blue Boy*, is non-fungible because there is not another painting of its type in existence.
Non-fungible token	A unique cryptographic asset which exists on a blockchain. It has distinctive metadata and identification codes that identify other blockchain tokens. While it is unique from other types of tokens it may be sold and exchanged, but its unique features mean that no two tokens are alike.
Personal Identification Number	Referred to as a PIN or by some as a PIN Number. The purpose of the PIN is to facilitate the exchange of private data. PINs are widely used between an individual and an institution such as a governmental body, bank, or financial institution, particularly when making card payments, i.e. a credit, or debit card. A PIN can also be issued to an individual to be used digitally. These digital PINs can be used to authenticate the user's identity to access a platform, application or website.
Quasi-digital asset	An asset which is digital in nature, but which also exists in a traditional environment. A quasi-digital asset has three common defining features. The first is that it has a binary existence and uses a digital access gateway. Secondly, that any right associated with it is not absolute but is often reliant upon a third party or is subservient to a third party's rights or conditions. Thirdly, there is an alternative method of access that permits one to bypass the digital access gateway.
Social media	Interactive technological web-based applications, or platforms that facilitate the creation and sharing of information, ideas, interests, themes or other forms of expression through networks, virtual communities and groups. Individuals, businesses and organisations are able to create,

share, co-create, discuss, participate and modify user-generated or self-curated content online using social media. Social media can also be used to document memories; learn about and explore things; advertise oneself; and form relationships and friendships.

Vlog A video blog similar in many regards to a blog in terms of individual or small group maintenance. A vlog may be a standalone web page or website or it may operate through a media platform such as YouTube or Vimeo. As with a newspaper's editorial page, the information is normally opinion-based, but there is a trend with vlogs to be educational and/or themed, i.e. based around topics. An excellent example of the vlog concept is that of young women's struggle with Non-Hodgkin lymphoma, available on YouTube.[1]

---

1 Kimberly-Ann Debling, 'Kim's Channel', YouTube, www.youtube.com/channel/UCo-HDr2z_ rCi9g7ijeLOUig; 'Harrowing photos …', *Daily Mail*, 3 May 2018, www.dailymail.co.uk/health/article-5685851.

Part 2
General Considerations

1 Defining Digital Assets

1.1 What are digital assets (financial and non-financial)?

In 2018, *Forbes* magazine reported that a 7-year-old boy named Ryan Kaji earned an estimated £28.6 million reviewing toys on YouTube, making him the highest paid YouTube influencer of 2018.[1] McAfee's Global survey in 2013 found that the average individual has US$35,000 of value stored on their mobile devices,[2] and over the last 7 years it is likely that that value has only increased.

While many people are not in the same league as Ryan Kaji, many of us now have a diverse number of online accounts which create a digital presence. This expanding digital web presence includes social media profiles, blogs or vlogs, online accounts for gambling, crowd funding, share payment apps such as Venmo, banking, pensions and investments such as shares, peer-to-peer lending or crypto-currencies. A significant amount of value may be tied up in online accounts that is not readily accessible to immediate family or the personal representatives and/or executors on the account holder's death. An excellent example of how not to deal with digital assets was reported in *The Guardian* newspaper.[3] The untimely death in December 2018 of Gerald Cotten, a 30-year-old crypto-currency exchange executive, who left no instructions on how to access his US$150 million crypto-currency digital assets, deprived his relatives of those assets. Almost 4 years later, his account remains impenetrable, with US$150 million effectively consigned to the digital scrap heap.

Within the last two decades digital assets have become an integral part of our modern life, and this has only accelerated during the COVID-19 pandemic.[4] Digital assets are present in our personal, professional and

---

1 'How this 7-year-old made $22 million playing with toys', *Forbes*, 3 December 2018, www.forbes.com.

2 'More than 30% of people don't password protect their mobile devices', McAfee Blog, 24 February 2013, www.mcafee.com.

3 'Investors who lost $190m demand exhumation of crypto-currency mogul', *The Guardian*, 13 December 2019, www.theguardian.com.

4 Ofcom reported that, during June 2020, adults spent a record 25% of their waking time online. 'UK's internet use surges to record levels', Ofcom, 24 June 2020, www.ofcom.org.uk.

family lives, but what happens to them when we die or cease to have sufficient mental capacity to operate them? Clearly, as with any chattel or traditional asset class, we must plan for what happens to our digital assets on death or when we lose mental capacity, as digital assets can have either a financial value or a sentimental value or both. Importantly, before we consider the probate and planning aspects of digital assets, we should consider what is and what is not a digital asset.

Digital assets are often considered to be anything that exists in a binary form with an associated right of use. It is the combination of the binary form and the associated right that differentiates a digital asset from simply being a digital file or folder. This asset might exist on a computer hard drive, such as on a personal laptop, or its existence may be virtual, such as on a cloud service or similar shared third-party platform, but without the associated right, or 'permissions' as some computer scientists refer to them, it is not an asset. Examples of digital assets are digital documents, audible content, image content, motion imagery files, tokens, blogs, vlogs, websites, online gaming and domain names. These include a diverse range of digital content from crypto-currencies and blockchain tokens such as bitcoin, ripple and ethereum, to YouTube content, Facebook profiles, digital holiday photographs and email.

It is often easier for the non-technically minded individual to identify a digital asset than to attempt to describe its binary attributes. One of the features of the technological field is that it is in a state of perpetual motion. This means that the formats and mediums are constantly changing and evolving, but in most cases the underlying data or purpose may be the same. For example, the 3½-inch floppy disc was the standard for PC computing in the early 1990s, which was then replaced by the CD-ROM, the USB flash drive and cloud storage, all within a 25-year time period. While the storage device may have become outdated, the digital photographic image stored on that 3½-inch floppy drive is still present, and still has a value which may be financial or purely sentimental. If one has the technology to read (or transfer) that digital photographic image, it can be passed on to another person, such as a family member. This shows how portable certain digital assets can be, providing one has the technology to access the binary data on the storage device or – in common parlance – to access the data file.

It is possible to classify digital assets into two groups – those with a financial value and those with sentimental value. Clearly, some digital assets may have a financial value based upon the content and this then causes them to cross from the sentimental value group to having a financial value. A good example of a truly sentimental digital asset would be a family photograph stored on a USB flash drive. Remember here that the 'asset' is not the physical USB flash drive, but the image file stored on the drive. An example of a digital asset that straddles the financial and sentimental value groups might be a photograph taken by the deceased of a celebrity person. It can have a sentimental value to the photographer or the other persons in the image. It might also have a financial value to the tabloid press regardless of whether it is stored on a celluloid or in a digital file format. More particularly, it is the right to reproduce or license the image which is valuable over the simple possession of the image. In this example it is the photographic content, or specific rights associated with it, that is generating value and not the actual digital file itself. This is an excellent example of how a digital asset can have both a financial value and a sentimental value, and how the digital file and associated legal rights and interest come together.

In the traditional non-digital probate system, it is easy to draw a line between financial matters and sentimental matters. In a non-digital probate, one would settle out the bank accounts, stocks, shares, life insurances and real estate and count them and their associated values as part of the estate valuation process. The inventory of contents would then be made and that would usually include assets of a more sentimental nature. In the digital sphere, we have digital assets that equally divide between assets of value and sentimental items of trivial financial value. It is less easy to draw a clear distinction between an individual's digital assets and their quasi-digital assets. In order to establish clarity, one must consider where those binary files – such as digital documents, subscriptions, licences, audible content, image content, motion imagery files, tokens, blogs, vlogs, websites and online gaming tokens – that have insufficient rights to allow them to be truly considered as digital assets fall. They are clearly not traditional assets as they exist in a digital environment, but the lack of the associated right means that they fail the digital asset test. They therefore fall into a 'halfway house'-like state of a quasi-digital asset.

1.2 What are quasi-digital assets?

In the same way that some digital assets will straddle the definition of financial and sentimental, there are also assets that fall between the definitions of traditional and digital assets, or at the very least blur the edges of those classes. These assets are digital in nature, but also exist in a traditional environment. An excellent example of this is the online bank account. The account is accessible online, but there is a methodology which allows the account to be accessed in a traditional probate manner. It is not only 'bricks and mortar' banks' online accounts that exist in this quasi-digital asset class, but also digital payment platforms' accounts, such as PayPal, Venmo and their stable-mates. Quasi-digital assets have common defining features, which include the following:

- a binary existence using a digital access gateway;
- any associated right is not absolute, but is often reliant upon a third party;
- an alternative method of access that permits one to bypass the digital access gateway.

The last feature above is in direct contrast to a true digital asset where access can only be achieved through a digital access gateway. The most obvious example of this is a crypto-currency, such as bitcoin, which can only be accessed through the keycode/password combination and a PayPal account. Losing or misplacing the logon information to a PayPal account does not mean that the funds are lost. There are other methods that one can use to gain access. Access is, after all, controlled centrally by PayPal. This contrasts enormously with the bitcoin example where there is no central controlling board that can allow third party access.

Individuals may spend significant amounts of money on the acquisition of a quasi-digital asset or the content related to a quasi-digital asset account. As with a physical asset, the amount of money expended on a quasi-digital asset may not correlate to a valuable post-death asset. Certain accounts are by their very nature non-transferable and are personal licences to the individual account holder. Accounts such as Amazon Prime Video, Amazon E-Books, Audible, Flickr, iTunes and Spotify utilise a licenser/licensee relationship. This means that the individual end user does not actually purchase a song, ebook, movie or digital file, but rather the platform provider permits the end user the right to use the content subject to the platform provider's terms and conditions. This means that, despite the significant expense to create an extensive iTunes music library, on death the library simply evaporates into the digital graveyard as the digital licence is non-transferable.

The legal concepts of copyright and licensing are often difficult to explain in simple terms to lay people. As probate professionals, we should endeavour to translate the complex issues into understandable concepts. Analogies often assist us and, in relation to the quasi-digital asset, it often helps the lay person to separate the concept of the platform from the item. This leads neatly into the supermarket checkout conveyor belt analogy. At the supermarket, the customer places the items they wish to purchase on the checkout conveyor belt; these are scanned by the cashier and paid for by the customer; the purchased items are then placed in the customer's shopping bag. The same is true for a quasi-digital asset such as an iTunes account or an Amazon Prime digital content. The Apple iTunes application is, in essence, the supermarket conveyor belt; it is equipment which is owned by Apple in the same way the supermarket owns the checkout conveyor belt. The song or tune that the customer downloads is the item to be purchased and the shopping bag is the iTunes Library. The term 'library' is useful in assisting the lay person's understanding of the quasi-digital asset landscape, for just as with a public lending library where one has to return the items checked out upon death of the library card holder, the same applies to the digital content. This breakdown of the competing legal rights, the legal framework and technology may be seen by some as an over-simplification, but one of the greatest responsibilities of the professional probate adviser is to give the lay client a comfortable level of understanding. Ignorance is not bliss and it has the potential to be harmful.

1.3 Digital pathways – defining the lines

As already discussed, there is a distinction between digital assets and quasi-digital assets. There is also the concept of a 'digital pathway'. The digital pathway is the avenue to access those digital and/or quasi-digital assets. The digital pathway might be related to a particular username/password combination that allows one to access the digital asset. It might be a piece of hardware or device such as an iPhone, iPad, tablet or laptop. A piece of hardware and a device are both a traditional asset (as it has a commercial value as a piece of hardware) and also have a value as a digital pathway.

As probate professionals, it is important to make enquiries of the client to uncover the extent to which the client has, and utilises, digital assets. It is equally important that enquiries are made as to which digital pathways the client uses to access their digital assets. It is not simply enough to assume that clients of a particular age or generational profile do not have digital assets or have complex digital pathways. Certain individuals, particularly in the age-bracket that is 65 and older, have made significant leaps in 2020 to expand their digital footprint. One of the impacts of the COVID-19 pandemic is that individuals aged 65-plus, who were encouraged to self-isolate, expanded their digital footprint as a matter of necessity. There was a significant shift to digital shopping, home delivery and digitalised social activities, such as bridge clubs, moving to an online format. Every digital shopping account and every username/password combination gives rise to a digital pathway and a potential digital asset or quasi-digital asset. While the concepts of digital asset and digital pathways have existed for some years, society's recent acceleration into creating a greater digital footprint means that it is essential to make sufficient enquiries into a client's usage of, and footprint in, the digital world.

As with any journey, the best course of action is to identify and define the landscape on the map before packing the car. It is important for us to help clients understand that their digital footprint matters to their estate planning process. When considering the potential for digital assets and digital pathways, it is important to note that not all digital pathways lead to digital assets or quasi-digital assets. On some occasions the digital asset may be of little or nominal value, or the digital pathway may simply lead to a dead end.

An ideal way to uncover digital assets and digital pathways is to utilise a client questionnaire. In the same way that we might use a questionnaire to enquire about real property and a client's family relationships, a client questionnaire allows clients to document their digital footprint. The value of the client questionnaire is to provide a starting point for conversations with the client. The client questionnaire is doubly useful as it helps practitioners to adopt a systematic approach towards digital assets and digital pathways, which is useful as it ensures that topics are not omitted from the client conversation. Having a completed document in the client's own hands is also useful as both an *aide-mémoire* and in the event of a *Larke v Nugus*[5] request. A client questionnaire has many uses. At one level, it is simply a starting point for the conversations regarding the client's digital footprint and pathways. At another level, it is to direct an open dialogue with the client regarding their digital asset security pattern. Another dimension in which the client questionnaire can be used is in leading a conversation regarding how much of that digital footprint they wish to remain after their death, or to whom and in what manner they wish their digital assets to be distributed or dealt with after their death. The options will range from having accounts deleted to appointing an individual to administer their portfolio of digital assets and quasi-digital assets. That individual may receive the digital assets as a gift or they may simply be there to manage the digital assets for the benefit of the estate.

It is possible for the deceased to appoint an individual specifically to deal with their digital assets. This individual is commonly known as a digital executor or digital administrator. The term digital executor can be confusing as this individual may or may not be the personal representative and/or executor of the rest of the client's estate. With the advent of the HM Courts & Tribunals Service processing grants of probate electronically, it is also easy to see why the term 'digital executor' could be misconstrued. The term 'digital administrator' is preferable as it more accurately defines the responsibilities and obligations of the role. It also means that there can be a clear distinction between the rights and responsibilities of traditional executorship and administering to a client's digital assets, quasi-assets and digital footprint.

There is presently no distinction within probate proceedings to make specific grants to a digital administrator. Grants of probate should be

---

5 [1979] 123 Sol Jo 337.

made to the personal representative and/or executor. The digital administrator can and should be named within the client's last will and testament. The particular actions and profile/account information relating to the digital footprint can be set out in a statement of wishes or incorporated into the last will and testament. It would also be possible to draft a codicil to an existing last will and testament to include the appointment of a digital administrator. Samples of draft clauses for the appointment of a digital administrator can be found at Appendix A1.

1.4 Summary – digital assets and quasi-digital assets

While we have considered in detail defining the qualities and features of the digital and quasi-digital asset, not every client will own both types of assets. In most cases, the client will own some of one type and none of the other type.

Many practitioners make assumptions, as the author is all too aware, of the technical abilities of our clients. Independent research[6] has shown that the COVID-19 pandemic has accelerated internet and device use by seniors. As of 2020 almost 70% of seniors used their smartphones for accessing social networks, which is a substantial increase over the 43% in 2016. The same research study shows that 17% of seniors use their smartphones for online shopping and 66% use the internet simply to browse.[7] This data demonstrates a clear need for practitioners to be familiar with the concepts and trends amongst their clients. Almost 2 billion people worldwide will fall into the senior definition over the next 25 years,[8] and this category is known as the 'aging techies' generation. This generation is one that grew up with the digital revolution, the Apple and Commodore home computers. On the whole, they have continued to embrace the digital advances and, as the research demonstrates, they continue to embrace and adapt to evolving digital technology. It is unlikely these trends will change as they go through retirement.[9]

---

6 Ericsson ConsumerLab, 'Seniors and technology during Covid-19: the latest insights', Ericsson, 26 January 2021, www.ericsson.com.

7 Ericsson ConsumerLab, 'Seniors and technology during Covid-19: the latest insights', Ericsson, 26 January 2021, Figure 5, www.ericsson.com.

8 The projected increase of seniors in society. Source: United Nations, Department of Economic and Social Affairs, Population Division, *World Population Ageing 2019: Highlights* (ST/ESA/SER.A/430) (United Nations, 2019).

9 Ericsson ConsumerLab, 'Seniors and technology during Covid-19: the latest insights', Ericsson, 26 January 2021, www.ericsson.com.

When dealing with clients, the following may serve as an *aide-mémoire* to the most commonly used digital and quasi-digital assets. Helpfully, the appropriate cross-reference is included following each of the asset classes.

1.5 Commonly held digital assets

- Crypto-currency and associated tokens (such as non-fungible tokens) (see 9.1 onwards).
- Digital image files, such as digital photos (see 5.2).
- Digital media files, such as digital video (see 1.4).
- Digital written files, such as Microsoft Word (Word) documents, spreadsheets, Microsoft Notepad (Notepad) files, Adobe Portable Document Format (PDF) files (see 3.4 and 6.7).
- Digital presentations, such as Microsoft PowerPoint (PowerPoint) presentations (see 3.4 and 6.7).
- HTML documents (see 6.7).
- Social media content (Facebook, Twitter, Instagram, LinkedIn, Snapchat) (see 10.4 to 10.10).
- Vlogs (YouTube, TikTok, Vimeo) (see 6.3).
- Blogs (see 6.9).
- Websites and/or domain names (see 10.12).
- Online gaming accounts and/or National Lottery accounts (see 6.13 and 6.14).

1.6 Commonly held quasi-digital assets

- Online membership/subscriptions (Amazon Prime, Netflix) (see 2.15 and 6.15).
- Digital content providers (Amazon content such as Prime Video, Audible/ebooks, iTunes, Spotify, etc) (see 2.2).
- Online payment accounts (Google Pay, Apple Pay, Venmo, PayPal, etc) (see 8.3 and 12.1).
- Merchant selling accounts (eBay, Amazon Marketplace, etc) (see 6.15).
- Online purchasing accounts (eBay, Amazon, etc) (see 6.15).

Part 3
Pre-death Issues

2 Considerations when Advising the Testator

> Before anything else, preparation is the key to success.
>
> Alexander Graham Bell

The advisory aspect of the probate practitioner's work can be extremely rewarding. It offers an opportunity for client education, inter-generational planning and inter-disciplinary work with tax professionals. These preparatory discussions afford an opportunity for practitioners to learn about individual clients' digital footprints and their respective digital assets and quasi-digital assets. It is important for the probate practitioner to both educate and be educated by the client.

There are many aspects of life which now take place in the digital environment. Clients in most cases do not comprehend the extent of their digital footprint or the impact it has on their estate. Equally, they may not comprehend the matters that need to be considered or the actions that need to be taken. It is also easy for the client to underestimate the amount of work that needs to be undertaken when dealing with digital assets.

In order to ensure that all areas of the client's digital footprint are explored it is important to approach the topic in a systematic fashion. There are a number of areas where information gathering should be concentrated; these core areas are financial digital assets, social media and non-financial digital assets. A discussion of the client's digital footprint will likely start with a conversation about their most frequently used social media platforms, such as Facebook, LinkedIn, Twitter, etc, and then cover non-financial digital assets, such as Dropbox, online banking, followed by purely digital financial assets, such as crypto-currency. Progressing through these areas in a systematic way will ensure that no stone is left unturned. In order to assist in these discussions, a checklist may be made available to the lay client for them to complete in advance of any in-person meeting. A suitable checklist can be found at Appendix A2.

2.1 Memorandum of wishes, also known as a letter of wishes

A memorandum of wishes, or letter of wishes, can be particularly useful when dealing with digital assets. Traditionally used by some practitioners to dispose of chattels or items of personal property, the letter of wishes is very versatile. It is, of course, a non-legally binding document and is often considered as a set of instructions or guidelines. The public nature of probate means that the contents of the will eventually become public; a letter of wishes is confidential in nature and does not have to become public.

A more detailed letter of wishes could be useful in cases where a digital manager or digital executor is used. In this case it could be used as a series of instructions for the management of the digital content or digital assets.

In cases which are less onerous, instructions may be set out in a memorandum of wishes to cover a host of possibilities such as the memorialisation of social media accounts, maintenance of cloud accounts and issues relating to other digital accounts. There are several advantages to adopting a memorandum of wishes, including the ability to keep the matters confidential. Clearly, one would not want to make public in a will details of one's online transactions or digital assets. One advantage is that there is a versatility and flexibility in using a memorandum of wishes. Such a document can be written and re-written without having to conform to the formalities of a will. Another advantage is that the document can be prepared by the testator and there is no requirement to have it created by a legal practitioner. While these are the advantages, one must also consider the disadvantages. A memorandum of wishes is in many cases an appeal to the good graces and faith of the individual persons appointed as executor, digital executor or digital manager. It is in essence an appeal to them to bring these actions into effect. If the executor, digital executor or digital manager elects not to carry out the specific instructions or follow, or otherwise ignore, the sentiments expressed in a memorandum of wishes, there is little recourse. In reality, this is one of the most significant downfalls of such an approach. By contrast, if the matters are set out in the testator's last will and testament, there are more substantive safeguards. It must be remembered that executors hold legal duties to exercise caution and skill[1] and fiduciary obligations[2] including a legal duty of care.[3] For many years, practitioners would prefer to create a last will and testament that would be relatively short and accompany it with a letter of wishes or memorandum of

1 *Speight v Gaunt* (1883) 9 App Cas 1 at 19.

2 Trustee Act 1925, section 15 and Trusts of Land and Appointment of Trustees Act 1996, section 15.

3 Trustee Act 2000, section 1.

wishes. The letter of wishes or memorandum of wishes would dispose of personal chattels and/or paraphernalia. If a testator's digital assets and/or quasi-digital assets relate solely to non-financial affairs, it is appropriate to leave instructions via a letter of wishes or memorandum of wishes. This could reference topics such as how to dispose of digital photographs, hardware and devices, or personal digital files that had a wider impact, such as those relating to family history or genealogical research.

Where an individual has a more detailed inventory of financially valuable digital assets, it may be prudent to consider alternative arrangements. For example where an individual holds crypto-currency, it may be disposed of in the last will and testament as a specific legacy, or to a trust. Crypto-currency market pricing is very volatile, and those fluctuations can be significant. For example in 2010 one bitcoin was worth US$0.08, in 2021 the same token was valued at over US$50,000, and by August 2022 it was worth approximately US$19,800. Those fluctuations are in one of the most widely traded and recognised crypto-currency tokens, in less widely traded tokens the volatility can be more significant. Where there is the potential for such volatility and the accumulation or maintenance of such wealth, the prudent approach is to provide greater safeguards. The duties placed upon executors provide greater safeguards for beneficiaries and will ensure that the distribution of financially valuable digital assets is done in accordance with the testator's wishes, while providing beneficiaries a legal recourse.

Where a will establishes testamentary trusts or specific legacies for digital assets, a letter of wishes does not need to be excluded. The two approaches are not mutually exclusive. A disposition of financially valuable digital assets may be done using a trust or legacy under a will, but a letter of wishes may still be relevant for providing directions for dealing with personal non-financial digital assets such as social media accounts and emails, or such as photographs, videos or personal files.

An alternative use for a letter of wishes is to identify an individual's digital assets, as opposed to a using a digital asset inventory or client checklist. As a private document – rather than a public will proved in probate proceedings – the individual could include details of the digital assets, wallet, profiles and location of authentication devices, documents or software knowing that the document would always be private and not open to public inspection. This approach may be appropriate where the volume of information is relatively small and can be concisely contained within a single document.

A further discussion of this subject with particular reference to drafting can be found at 4.6. Appendix A3 also contains a precedent for a letter of wishes dealing with a settlor's crypto-currency and financially valuable digital assets.

2.2 Amazon – considerations to be made by account holders in advance

2.2.1 Background

Amazon has become a Behemoth of the digital age. Its size, scale and reach are almost unparalleled when compared with any other digital platform company. Arguably, for many people it is simply a necessary if not essential part of their life. While not all Amazon's registered users will utilise all its services, most registered users – and a distinction here must be drawn between registered users and Prime Membership users – will use at least two of them. As with all digital platforms, registered users became more dependent upon it during the COVID-19 pandemic and it is likely that this behaviour to a significant extent will survive into the post-pandemic normalcy. It is therefore essential that registered users and Prime Membership users understand both the limitations and the scope of dealing with their account after death.

Until 2021, there were limited ways of dealing with the death of an Amazon user irrespective of whether or not the deceased was a standard registered user or an Amazon Prime user. The terms and conditions governing both of those memberships made it clear that all content was the product of a licence between the individual user and Amazon, and that on the death of the Amazon user all rights attributable to the owner simply ceased. As a consequence of this interpretation, whole collections of ebooks, videos, photos and associated digital content were simply erased from the deceased user's account. This invariably led to numerous complaints, and claims were issued against Amazon primarily in the United States.

The most recent case, *Caudel v Amazon Inc*,[4] brought in the US Federal Court, alleged that the digital content in Amazon Prime digital video format was purchased and the title transferred to the registered user. This is based upon the issue of an advertising claim made by Amazon in its marketing of the digital content. Amazon offers two distinct options, one of which is to rent the digital video content for a fixed period of time, normally 24 or 48 hours. In essence, this is the same type of transaction that a customer would engage in with a 1980s video rental shop, namely a contract for the short-term use of an object in return for rent. The other option Amazon presents to its customers is to 'buy' the content, which is then available for an indefinite period of time. The position made by the

4 US District Courts, 2:20-CV-00848, 24 April 2020.

claimant in *Caudel v Amazon Inc*, is that the option to buy is clearly distinct from the option to rent as the language adds an air of permanence to the transaction. The position set out in Amazon's defence is that the contractual position clearly states it is an issue of licensing the film or other digital content from Amazon to the end user. Amazon's position is that the contract cannot be one of sale to the end user as Amazon itself cannot give a higher title than it already holds to the digital content. Amazon is licensed by the film copyright owner or distributor, it does not own the digital content outright, and therefore it cannot give ownership as it never had such an ownership title to give. The case was issued in 2020 and is still to reach its final determination.

The issues in the case are of interest as there are significant similarities to the physical possession of content recorded upon a video tape. In the video tape example, the individual in physical possession may not duplicate, reproduce or show the content to a commercial audience without infringing the artist's copyright ownership. An individual company may rent the video tape for a specific period of time to third parties, providing there is an agreement with the artist or the copyright's owner or agent which permits such actions by the company. While the technology may be digital, the legal rights can easily be applied from twentieth-century analogue video technology. The humble video tape and the associated video rental business may not have survived into the second decade of the twenty-first century, but the legal principles and framework that underpinned its business are very relevant to the Amazon digital content library.

2.2.2 Possible preparation actions

When discussing Amazon with the lay client, it is important to determine what the testator's Amazon usage is and whether or not they are taking maximum advantage of the Amazon Prime membership. It is perfectly possible that they may only have Amazon Prime without using many of the services Amazon provides. For example, clients may subscribe to Amazon Prime simply to get discounted delivery, whereas others may also use the full range of services such as Amazon Photo, Amazon E-Books, Amazon Prime Music, Amazon Prime Video and Amazon Games.

In the event that the client is only using the shopping features of Amazon, the account simply needs to be closed on the death of the registered user. For clients who are using multiple services from Amazon, there is a feature which allows the transfer of data and information to a family or household member. Crucially, this must be set up in advance of the Amazon Prime member's death and cannot be done *post mortem*. This type of transfer is done through a tool known as Amazon Household. This service allows up to two adults and four children to pool their Amazon digital content across the multiple Amazon services. It requires both adults to maintain separate Amazon Prime memberships and then they effectively pool their Amazon digital assets.

This pooling of Amazon-based digital content allows individuals to share content and, crucially, access independently irrespective of the device. For example, John Smith may access digital video content paid for by Jane Smith (and therefore licensed to her) from Amazon via his Fire TV Stick, and Jane Smith may access digital music content paid for by John Smith (and therefore licensed to him) from Amazon via his Fire Tablet.

Without this type of pooling there are limited options for those individuals with significant Amazon-based digital content. There is no other way to leave, share or transfer this type of content. Amazon users must understand that any digital content which they purchase on an Amazon platform is only a personal licence, which is non-transferrable. It is vital that the client is aware of these options and the steps that must be taken to set up and share content through the Amazon Household tool.

2.3 Google

2.3.1 Considerations to be made by account holders in advance

Google began originally as a search engine, but in the same way that Amazon began life as an online bookshop and then grew into a Behemoth, Google has done something similar. Google users have the ability to store data using Google services such as Gmail, and One Drive. Fortunately, Google provides a solution to the issue of passing stored digital data and content onto a beneficiary. The solution in the Google world is known as Google Inactive Account Manager. This allows a Google user to elect individuals to access and manage their content after a period of inactivity. This is particularly useful as the inactive period does not necessarily have to be one of death. It could simply be a true period of inactivity or it may be reflective of a period of disability or infirmity.

There are a number of scenarios where the Google Inactive Account Manager can play a beneficial role in assisting the probate practitioner. The first use is precisely because it is designed to notify a third party as to the existence of the account and the fact that it has not been used within a set number of days. This period can be as short as 90 days or as long as 12 months. The options are:

(a) to send a pre-arranged message to a maximum of 10 contacts;

(b) to provide permission for a maximum of 10 contacts to access and download the Google content;

(c) to delete the entire account and all related Google data.

The pre-arranged email message to pre-appointed email contacts is very useful as it allows information to be shared in the event of mental disability, physical infirmity or death. The content is decided by the Google user and could include reference to a Personal Identification Number (PIN), or a username and password combination. In this manner the Google Inactive Account Manager may be used as a dead man's switch, although this may be too basic and insecure for the more sophisticated type of client.

Secondly, the ability to download and provide access to specific data from Google is significant for both clients and probate practitioners and/or executors. For some clients this may be an appropriate method for them to share their entire digital footprint from photographs and PDF and Word documents to emails. The Google user is able to specify which elements of Google data are shared with the pre-authorised contacts. Therefore, it is possible to keep information such as browser history entirely private whilst sharing all the Gmail content.

Thirdly, for some clients, the Google Inactive Account Manager is simply a convenient way to ensure that all their Google data is deleted after death. This can be an effective strategy from a time management and administrative cost perspective. In the event that the client wishes to delete all their Google data then the probate practitioner and/or executor should highlight the benefits of this approach to the client. Clients should be aware that once this strategy is initiated it 'crosses the Rubicon' and the data deleted through Google Inactive Account Manager is lost forever. In order to select this option, the Google user needs to make that election by specifying the number of days to elapse before the account is considered inactive and deletion can then take place.

It should be noted in all these cases that the Google Inactive Account Manager will not activate when there is an active Gmail or Google account linked to a mobile phone. This is because the account will continue to send and receive messages from the mobile phone. The inactivity period often begins when the phone is turned off or placed into a state of suspension.

It also needs to be noted that the Google Inactive Account Manager does not erase any data held locally on a hard drive or a device. It only deals with data stored on Google's cloud platforms. This means that browser history and other data may still remain on a mobile phone or tablet even after the Google data has been deleted on the cloud platform.

The probate practitioner therefore needs to obtain clear instructions on the precise option that the individual wishes to elect. It must be remembered that it is not possible to pass a Google account or a Gmail account by a will or other testamentary document to a third party. The Google Inactive Account Manager is the only option available. In most cases, as a minimum the client is likely to nominate an individual or individuals to receive all the associated data. This data can be particularly helpful in managing an estate, especially if the individual was using their email account for the payment of bills and/or subscriptions, as the information relating to those accounts will show up and provide the information needed to settle any such outstanding matters.

2.4 Creating a letter of wishes with digital assets, particularly social media, in mind

A letter of wishes can also be useful for identifying the settlor's social media profile names and email protocols. These may change over time, and the editable nature of a letter of wishes means that it can be a cohesive living document, as opposed to a will that is often more stagnant, and less likely to be updated with the same frequency. This editable format allows for changes to be made by the lay client without the need for professional assistance. Since the letter of wishes is designed to be editable in nature, changes made to it by the lay client do not bring into question its legal validity.

There is no standard letter of wishes for collating and dealing with a settlor's social media, but it should follow a format similar to a letter of wishes in relation to nil rate bands and life interest matters. The letter should declare upon its face that it is a letter of wishes and that it is not legally binding on the personal representatives and/or executors. As with all letters of wishes, there should be multiple copies made of the document. One copy should be placed with the testator's will, other copies should be deposited with the personal representatives and/or executors and one copy should be retained by the testator. The following wording may be used:

Letter of wishes

To the Executors and Trustees of my Last Will and Testament dated [*insert date],* [alternatively: Of this] the [*insert*] day of [*insert month and year*].[5]

In this letter, I set out my wishes with regard to my digital assets, with particular reference to my social media, which you have powers to deal with under my Will. These wishes set out in this document are not legally binding upon you and are intended as a guide as to my personal wishes.

Once the letter of wishes heading and opening has been set out, the substance of the letter of wishes can include the testator's passwords management software/provider, computer hardware information/locations, website logins, PIN, password reset information, email account addresses, social media accounts, file hosting services, blog/vlog information, legacy contact and memorialisation information. The benefit of the letter of wishes is that it can be as comprehensive as the writer desires. In some cases, it may be all-encompassing, including information relating to the what, where and how of the individual accounts held. In other cases, it may simply set out the broad intention of the writer to have social media accounts terminated on death and identify how the personal representatives and/or executors should deal with related matters.

2.5 Advising the client in relation to social media

It will come as no surprise that social media providers have not placed a direct focus on the death aspect of users. Every social media platform has a slightly different approach to the subject of users and death. There is no unified process on dealing with the death of a user, but there is commonality in the approaches used by each of the social media providers. In order to advise the lay client about the options available to them, it is important to understand the approach of each provider. It is important to note that in some cases there are a number of choices and there are decisions that need to be made in advance of death.

5 In the event that the letter of wishes is designed to replace an existing letter of wishes or is written much later than the date of the last will and testament, the letter of wishes should bear the date it is made.

2.6 What are the social media options?

2.6.1 The deletion option

There are two general approaches to social media accounts on the death of the registered user. The first is to have the account deleted and the second is to have the account maintained in some way, shape or form. Deletion is an important step as it protects the deceased user's data and their contacts from being exposed to possible illicit criminal activity. It is therefore imperative that there is a coherent approach to social media accounts because to allow one or more accounts to become dormant or inactive risks allowing the criminal element in society to exploit it. No matter what account or accounts the testator is using, deletion on death is, and always remains, an option open to all users. However, it is an option that needs careful consideration as there can be a vast amount of data, such as images, videos and interactions, kept in some social media accounts. Since most of that data is held remotely on a social media cloud-based platform, it is unlikely to exist in its entirety in another location. Therefore, deletion may mean that all that data are lost. The lay client should understand that deletion of social media accounts will completely eliminate all the data in the account including images, conversations and videos.

2.6.2 The memorialisation option

This option allows the account to be placed in a form of suspension which is then monitored or maintained by a third party. The third party is appointed by the user prior to death, and in most cases the option must be elected by the user before death. Memorialisation is dealt with differently by every social media provider. The basic concept is the same but the functionalities are different. This means that in almost all cases the user's profile remains online, with a limited amount of data. In some cases, the authorised third party is entitled to download the data and, in other cases, this is not permitted.

2.6.3 Alternative options to deletion and memorialisation

While the most common situations in social media for the testator to elect are either memorialisation or deletion there are social media applications which adopt a slightly different approach. The most common of these are Twitter and LinkedIn, and the process for each is as follows.

Twitter

Twitter is the world's largest micro blogging site. It limits almost all users to short messages of 140 characters or less. These messages are known as 'Tweets' and can contain imagery and words. Tweets can be seen by other users on Twitter's site and the public at large. Twitter does not presently offer a memorialisation service, so there are two options to consider when looking at a Twitter account belonging to a deceased user. The choice is between maintaining the account or deleting the account. Twitter allows immediate family members or a 'legally authorised individual' to contact it and request deletion. There is a form to complete and this can be found on the Twitter privacy page. A 'legally authorised individual' is identified on the privacy form simply as 'lawyer'. As a California-based company, Twitter uses the term 'lawyer' generically in its online forms. For the purposes in England and Wales, it applies to any legally qualified person who represents the interests of the estate or the interests of an incapacitated person. Upon completion of the online form, contact will be initiated by Twitter. At that time, copies of the grant of probate and/or enduring power of attorney should be supplied by email, depending upon the nature of the enquiry. Usefully, Twitter will accept an electronic copy of the deceased user's death certificate and is able to deactivate the account of a deceased user on receipt of the death certificate and notification from the next of kin. This is most helpful because it can be done upon receipt of the death certificate rather than waiting a significant period of time for the grant of probate to be issued. When reporting or request for deactivation is done by the next of kin or 'immediate family member', the individual concerned must provide evidence of their identity. This means providing personal information in the contact form such as name, address and date of birth, which is all subject to verification. In the follow-up email in response to the online form notification, an immediate family member must be ready to upload a proof of identity such as a passport or a driving licence should it be requested by Twitter. The data acquired by Twitter in these circumstances is used solely for the purposes of establishing the identity of the individual and their *locus standi* to be able to deal with the request to delete the deceased person's account. It is not used for any other purpose such as marketing or data mining.

Twitter is not able to allow anyone, including executors, lawyers or third parties, any access to the deceased user's actual account. The account will remain locked and Twitter will not share the login information. This inactive account status is exactly what some Twitter users wish to avoid, while for others it is exactly what they want to happen. In either event, it is important that one sets the appropriate expectation with the client.

LinkedIn

LinkedIn, pursuant to the LinkedIn User Agreement, operates a systematic deletion process of 'inactive' accounts. This means that an individual account will eventually be deleted after a significant period of inactivity. There are, however, alternatives that would allow a user's LinkedIn profile to be deleted.

The first is to delete the profile prior to death. Since this is an irreversible action, it is not one to be taken lightly.

The second is to provide the username and password to a trusted third party such as a digital administrator. The appointed individual can then log into the account and delete the profile. It should be noted that, strictly speaking, it is a breach of the LinkedIn User Agreement to share a username and password to allow a third party to access your LinkedIn profile. The penalty for permitting the third party access is termination of the account and deletion. There are risks with this approach as it allows the third party full access to the profile, data and personal information. This level of access allows the individual logging on to act as the registered user would, for example by reading and sending messages and communications, and viewing connections.

The third alternative is to leave instructions for a personal representative and/or executor to notify LinkedIn of the death. This does not require the personal representative and/or executor to have access to the account at all. There is a form to complete, which is available on the LinkedIn website. The individual notifying LinkedIn will need to provide the deceased user's full name, the nature of the notifier's relationship to the deceased, the deceased's email address (as registered with LinkedIn, which may be a work email address), the date of death, the name of the most recent company that the deceased worked for and a link to the obituary. Upon receiving that information, LinkedIn will take steps to remove the account from the platform. This may take days to complete and there may still be cached versions of the profile available through third-party search engines such as Google or Yahoo.

Detailed step-by-step instructions on how to deal with LinkedIn and Twitter post-death are set out at 10.7 and 10.10, respectively.

2.7 Pre-death considerations for crypto-currencies

The media abounds with apocryphal stories of 'lost' bitcoin or other crypto-currency coins. The most recent estimates indicate that approximately 20% of all existing 18.5 million bitcoins are lost or otherwise stranded.[6] That amounts to approximately 3.5 million individual bitcoin tokens. According to the rules set out by HM Revenue & Customs (HMRC) in its *Cryptoassets Manual*,[7] lost tokens or coins are not considered as a disposal for tax purposes. The rationale for this is that the token is not lost forever. The reason for the loss is the fact that the information required to access the crypto-token has been mislaid. The financial value of the password is minimal and of no financial value in and of itself. It therefore follows that lost usernames and passwords are not considered as a disposal for tax purposes even though the inaccessible asset protected by the password may hold a significant financial or taxable value. It is therefore critical to take steps to ensure that crypto-currencies are protected from loss.

There are a number of different approaches that an individual can take in relation to protecting crypto-currencies. The first thing to consider is how the crypto-currencies are stored. There are a number of possibilities, but in reality there are two main types: a software wallet and a hardware wallet. The first type of software wallet is an online digital wallet linked to an exchange for buying and selling crypto-tokens. It is designed to make buying, selling and transferring crypto-tokens easy. This means it is not the most secure of places to leave crypto-tokens for an extended period of time because, as with all software, it is connected to the internet and therefore susceptible to hacking and potential theft. There are software-based wallets that are not linked to exchanges, and these are often compared to online bank accounts. They operate in a similar manner using multiple layers of security, such as requiring a code or authentication system from a linked mobile phone to access the account in addition to the basic username and password combination. The risks associated with software wallets and exchange-linked wallets can be reduced by using a hardware wallet in addition to an exchange wallet. A hardware wallet might look similar to a USB drive and, to the untrained eye, can often be confused with a USB drive. The advantage with this type of wallet is that when it is not connected to the computer it is completely inert and cannot be hacked into. When a trade needs to be placed, the USB is connected to a computer and the information is transferred to the exchange wallet to facilitate the transaction.

Whichever method an individual uses for storing crypto-currencies needs to be noted so that personal representatives and/or executors are aware of the particular type of wallet used by the testator. The second matter to

---

6 'Lost passwords lock millionaires out of their bitcoin fortunes', *New York Times*, 21 January 2021.

7 HM Revenue & Customs, *Cryptoassets Manual*, at CRYPTO22100, 30 March 2021, www.gov.uk.

cover is how the personal representatives and/or executors are to obtain access to the digital wallet of choice. There are a number of options, the first of which is a written record of passwords. This would then need to be secured as it could be misused in the wrong hands. A second option is to have the digital wallet kept in a safe location, such as a safe deposit box, a personal safe or with a third party. This is particularly suited to hardware wallets in the form of USBs. A third option is for the matters to be set out in a statement, or memorandum of wishes, which is then lodged with the individual's solicitor for safe-keeping. A fourth option is for a dead man's switch to be established.

3 A Client Questionnaire – What One Might Look Like and How to Use It

For the probate practitioner there are many challenges when considering the digital aspects of the client's estate. One of the most concerning areas for any practitioner is the risk that the digital assets could be lost. There are a number of possible actions that could be taken to minimise the risk of loss of data and information, but the most useful strategy is to capture information from the client directly in the form of a comprehensive client questionnaire. This chapter considers how that client questionnaire might be put together and some of the questions that practitioners may wish to include.

3.1 The introduction

The opening paragraph should serve to introduce the form and the type of information requested as well as introducing the purposes of the questionnaire:

> The purpose of this form is to capture information related to your digital assets and digital habits. The purpose of this form is not to act as a record of usernames/passwords/PINs. The answers you provide in this questionnaire will be used to assist your executors in dealing with your estate on your death. These answers will also be helpful to your attorney or deputy in the event that you are incapable of dealing with your own affairs. It is important to be as detailed as possible when answering the questions in this questionnaire.

Clients can often misunderstand the purpose of such questionnaires, particularly if they are overly long or drafted in a verbose manner. It is therefore important for practitioners to use or devise forms that are both clear and concise. The suggested introduction seeks both clarity and precision.

3.2 How to format the client questionnaire

There is a temptation to make this client questionnaire a series of lengthy questions. It is acceptable, and possibly easier for the lay client to follow, to adopt a combination approach using both questions and tables. The tables can then be interspersed with questions, as further details will be required as well as additional space for clients to include their own personal notes.

Some of these tables may be an exercise in ticking boxes, such as in the following example:

Do you have any/use of the following platforms?

Platform	*Yes/No*	*Platform*	*Yes/No*
eBay		Skype	
Amazon		Microsoft Outlook	
Spotify		Zoom	
Twitter		YouTube	
Snapchat		Facebook inc./ Messenger	
Instagram		WhatsApp	
TikTok		PayPal	

If you answered 'yes' to any of the above, please fill out the Further Information Section.

3.3 Which categories to include in the client questionnaire?

One of the challenges around creating a digital asset questionnaire is which categories to include and how to organise them. The questionnaire document often becomes more functional if the categories are laid out thematically, with a similar format for each theme. Clearly, some clients may have more to document in one particular theme than others, and this is to be expected. The following list may be useful as one category has a natural connection to the preceding and succeeding categories.

1 Hardware (computing devices, smartphones, smart watches, etc).

2 Smart home devices (Google Home, Amazon Alexa, Tado, etc and linked devices).

3 External storage (USBs, standalone or external hard drives, SD cards, flash drives).

4 Cloud storage (Google One Drive, Dropbox, etc).

5 Software (applications/apps, games, anti-virus, Microsoft Windows, Adobe suite and similar subscriptions).

6 Password vault or password manager (Lastpass, Bitwarden, 1Password, etc).

7 Email accounts.

8 Messaging accounts (WhatsApp, etc).

9 Social media platforms (Facebook, LinkedIn, etc).

10 Photo and video (Apple iCloud, Google Photos, Flickr, etc).

11 Video and blog platforms (Vimeo, YouTube, etc).

12 Streaming services (Netflix, Disney+, etc).

13 Ecommerce (eBay, Amazon Marketplace, etc).

14 Gambling and gaming accounts (National Lottery, Paddy Power, etc).

15 Mobile payment service and applications (PayPal, Apple Pay, Google Pay, etc).

16 Financial accounts (bank accounts, investments, crypto-currency, pensions).

17 Travel (Oyster card, train tickets, Expedia, etc).

18 Documents (PowerPoint presentations, Word and PDF documents, spreadsheets).

19 Other additional information (such as loyalty programmes, Airmiles, Tesco Clubcard, etc).

These 19 categories can then utilise a series of tables to record the relevant client information. These tables can follow a template such as the following example, which would be suitable for the first category.

1 Hardware (computing devices, smartphones, smart watches, etc)

Device	*Acer Laptop*
Device's normal location	*Office at home*
Ownership of the device/authorised users	*Bought by me new in 2018*
Protected access method (password/PIN)	*No Pin or password just turn it on to access it*
Linked accounts such as email/social media, etc	*MS Outlook on this device is linked to my Hotmail account. I don't use this for social media*
Is there a legacy contact/ beneficiary registered with the device/account?	*No. I want my executors to deal with it in accordance with my instructions on this form*
My wishes in relation to this device	*Leave it to my grandchildren Sam and Misha Smith*
Additional notes in relation to this device (Is there data to be removed? Should the device be destroyed?, etc)	*Remove my personal data and information before gifting it to my grandchildren*

The first sections of the table should be set out in the same way for all the categories, and the last two or three sections are also likely to be similar. There may be some changes to the mid-section as some of these categories may require greater or lesser details to enable the personal representatives and/or executors to have a useful picture of the testator's digital footprint.

9 Social media platforms (Facebook, LinkedIn, Twitter, etc)

Platform	*Facebook*
Device's normal location	*Smartphone (Samsung Galaxy S21)*
Ownership of the account/ authorised users	*I opened the account and I'm the only authorised user*
Protected access method (password/PIN/profile name)	*My Profile name is johnny.smith1983. The password is stored on my mobile app*
Linked accounts such as email/social media, etc (Which is the primary and the backup email	*The Facebook account is linked to my Hotmail account. My Gmail email address is registered as the backup email. My mobile*

account? Is there a mobile phone registered to the account?)	*phone number is also registered to my Facebook account.*
Is there a legacy contact/ beneficiary registered with the device/account?	*Yes my Facebook account has two legacy contacts appointed by me in 2021. They are my son James Smith and my cousin Rosemary Smith*
My wishes in relation to this account	*Memorialise the account and have it administered by the appointed legacy contacts*
Additional notes in relation to this device/account (Is there data to be removed? Should the device/ account be destroyed or deleted?, etc)	*I want the matter to be dealt with by my legacy contacts whom I've nominated through the Facebook app*

This demonstrates how the template can be versatile in its use and application. It is worth considering the changes that might be required when requesting information about accounts that are billed (whether it be annually, quarterly, monthly, or fortnightly) and which account the payment is coming from, such as the particular credit card, debit card or bank account.

15 Mobile payment service and applications (PayPal, Apple Pay, Google Pay, etc)

Platform	*PayPal*
Platform usual method of access	*Smartphone (Samsung Galaxy S21) and my laptop*
Ownership of the account/ authorised users	*I'm the only that is an authorised user*
Protected access method (password/PIN/username/ profile name)	*My username is johnny.smith1983. The password is stored in my password vault application*
Linked accounts such as email/social media, etc (Which is the primary and the backup email account? Is there a mobile phone registered to the account?)	*The PayPal account is linked to my Hotmail account. My Gmail email address is registered as the backup email. My mobile phone number and the password is stored in my safe*

Is there a legacy contact/ beneficiary registered with the device/account?	*No. There is no legacy contact/beneficiary on the account*
My wishes in relation to this account	*Transfer the account balance to my current account and distribute as part of my estate*
Additional notes in relation to this device/account (Are there any linked accounts? Is there data to be removed? Should the device/ account be destroyed or deleted?, etc)	*The PayPal account is linked to my NatWest current account*

3.4 Documents (such as PowerPoint presentations, Word and PDF documents, and spreadsheets)

When considering the issue of electronic documents, a number of questions should be asked in addition to the matters set out at the end of this section. It is highly probable that an individual may hold electronic copies of important documents on their devices, or in cloud-based applications. These require special consideration. Practitioners should note that electronic copies of certain documents have the same power as the originals. Electronic Communications Act 2000, section 7(1) states:

> (1) in any legal proceedings—
>
> (a) an electronic signature incorporated into or logically associated with a particular electronic communication or particular electronic data, and
>
> (b) the certification by any person of such a signature,
>
> shall each be admissible in evidence in relation to any question as to the authenticity of the communication or data or as to the integrity of the communication or data.

Electronic signatures are commonplace in commercial transactions, and when a practitioner uncovers an electronic document with an electronic signature, they should consider the significance of the contents and the rights and obligations set out in any and all such documents. Important rights and responsibilities may be uncovered and these may be valuable. An excellent example of an electronically signed document is the agreement between an Amazon Marketplace Merchant and Amazon. The contract provides for the terms of payment of storage fees, seller transaction and online payments. If the document were to be ignored, the estate may be liable for the payment of additional fees if the agreement is not terminated in line with the relevant clauses of the agreement. This could cause financial loss to the estate and difficulties between the personal representatives and/or executors and the beneficiaries and legatees.

One important consideration is to preserve such electronic documents to safeguard the rights of the individuals as the original copies of the documents may no longer exist. At the very least, caution should be taken to preserve such documents pending confirmation that the original document is in the personal representative's and/or executor's physical possession.

When considering electronic documents, the practitioner should note that not all electronically signed documents are legally binding. The most recent change in the concept of 'presence' in the context of a will[1] means that while signatures may be witnessed electronically, the signatures themselves must be physically attached to the last will and testament. The Wills Act 1837 (Electronic Communications) (Amendment) (Coronavirus) Order 2020[2] did not change the requirement for producing the original will in order to obtain a grant of probate, or the requirements for physically signing the document. It merely provided for the use of video conferencing and computer video technology in relation to the act of witnessing the signature of the testator; it does not make the signature an electronic signature. It should be noted that while these provisions were intended to end in January 2022, they have been extended by the Wills Act 1837 (Electronic Communications) (Amendment) Order 2022, with a revised end date of 31 January 2024.[3] This should allow sufficient time for further consideration of the role of technology in the signature process of documents such as wills. Following on from the Law Commission Report,[4]

---

1 Wills Act 1837, section 9(1) states that:

(1) No will shall be valid unless—

(a) it is in writing, and signed by the testator, or by some other person in his presence and by his direction; and

(b) it appears that the testator intended by his signature to give effect to the will; and

(c) the signature is made or acknowledged by the testator in the presence of two or more witnesses present at the same time; and

(d) each witness either—

(i) attests and signs the will; or

(ii) acknowledges his signature,

in the presence of the testator (but not necessarily in the presence of any other witness),

but no form of attestation shall be necessary.

2 SI 2020/952.

3 SI 2022/18.

4 *Electronic Execution of Documents*, Law Com No 386, 3 September 2019.

in March 2020, a multi-disciplinary team is actively undertaking work on this area. The Law Commission recommendation was that this work should consider the approach to deeds generally, the role of electronic documents and electronic signatures.

In the event that the practitioner or the lay executor uncovers electronic copies of testamentary documents, such as a revised last will and testament, consideration and further investigation may be warranted to trace the original document. The digital document may be the starting point for that further investigation and, clearly, such digital documents may be highly probative to such an investigation.

As discussed at 6.7 it is important to ask questions to uncover the ownership issue of electronic documents. It is possible that electronic documents might belong to the testator's employer, or the testator's limited company or perhaps a charity which the testator volunteers with. In these circumstances the documents will need to be read and either returned to the employer, the business or the charity. In the event that such documents relate to the testator's business it may be probative as to allow for the continuation of the testator's business or alternatively the effective winding up of the testator's business affairs on death.

It is therefore important to consider the following questions in relation to electronic documents in addition to a table approach for the reasons we have discussed in this section:

Documents (such as PowerPoint presentations, Word and PDF documents, spreadsheets)

Do you store any work files or documents on your personal devices? Yes/No

If so, what documents are they and where are they stored?

____

____

____

Do you store any files or documents on your personal devices which might relate to a charity or voluntary organisation that you are involved with? Yes/No

If so, what documents are they and where are they stored?

____

____

____

Do any of the files or documents stored on your personal devices relate to a business such as your own business or one in which you work with others whether in formal partnership or not? Yes/No

If so, what documents are they and where are they stored?

____

____

____

Do you have any system of formally and systematically backing up your electronic documents? Yes/No

If so, how are these backed up files accessed?

Type of location	*WD 3T external hard drive*
Protected access method (password/PIN/username/profile name)	*Files access is password protected using the PIN which my wife knows*
File details	*All my Word, PDF and Office documents are on this drive*
Any legal documents/correspondence? Or documents of sensitive or delicate nature?	*Copies of emails with my solicitor and draft copies of our wills. These are also copied on to my Gmail account*
Linked accounts such as a cloud platform providing backups for these files, etc (Where are the primary and backup accounts located?)	*The WD drive is backed up automatically to the MyCloud account. That backup is linked to my Gmail email address which is registered as the backup email. My mobile phone has the same PIN as the MyCloud account*
Is there a legacy contact/beneficiary registered with the device/account?	*No*
My wishes in relation to this account	*My wife and my son should be allowed to access the documents and decide what happens to these files*
Additional notes in relation to this device/account (Is there data to be removed? Should the files be destroyed or deleted?, etc)	

While every practitioner or firm can use these sample questions to create their own client questionnaire, for those who wish to see a completed version of the client questionnaire, an example is set out at Appendix A2.

4 Drafting Matters and Sample Will Clauses

> ... before writing his ninth symphony, Beethoven had a pretty good idea not merely of the legal theory of music, but as to the effect he was trying to create. No one is expecting you to produce statements of case of symphonic excellence (hopefully they will be somewhat shorter!), but the point still holds good. If you do not understand what you are trying to achieve the chances of ultimate success are slim.
>
> *Pleadings without Tears*, William Rose, 2002

There is much wisdom to be gleaned from that opening quote. Drafting and pleading are as much an art as writing a symphony or creating a sculpture. As with any art, there is a need to understand the end point and the context of the subject. There are times in the drafting of legal documents when a precedent is useful, but simply replicating precedents parrot-like, devoid of context and understanding, is to start walking on the footpath of failure.

This chapter explores sample forms of wording that can be used in conjunction with a practitioner's existing writing models. These draft clauses may be used together with other precedents, or combined with them, to create suitable documents. Practitioners are undoubtably all too aware of the inherent risks that drafting a will entails. The will drafter owes both duties to the testator and to the beneficiaries of the will.[1] It is therefore particularly important not only to consider the intentions of the testator, but also to bring them into effect in both a substantive and timely

---

1 *White v Jones* [1995] 2 AC 207 per Lord Goff at 260–290:

> In the forefront stands the extraordinary fact that, if [the claimed] duty is not recognised, the only persons who might have a valid claim (i.e. the testator and his estate) have suffered no loss, and the only person who has suffered a loss (i.e. the disappointed beneficiary) has no claim ... therefore ... if the solicitor owes no duty to the intended beneficiaries, there is a lacuna in the law which needs to be filled. This I regard as being a point of cardinal importance in the present case.

manner.[2] It is anticipated that the contents of this chapter will assist the practitioner in exercising 'the proper skill in preparation and execution of the will and with all due speed'.[3]

There are two documents where the draft clauses included in this chapter will be most helpful. The first is in the last will and testament and the second in the lasting power of attorney. It is also perfectly possible to apply these draft clauses to deeds, gifts and trusts; some minor amendments may be required, but these sample clauses should be the starting point for practitioners to develop their own symphonic drafting and linguistic style in the sphere of digital assets. The chapter starts by covering the draft clauses which may be most appropriate in a last will and testament setting.

4.1 Draft clauses for last will and testament

The key to drafting in a testamentary document is precision. If the wording is too particular or not precise enough, it is possible that the testator's wishes are not fully carried out or, worse, not carried out at all. An example of the former is:

> I give to Mr John Smith, of Blackacre Farm, all the money in my Alliance and Leicester Building Society Account 1234567.

Following the demutualisation and subsequent sale of the Alliance and Leicester Building Society to the Spanish bank, Santander, an element of tracing may be required to identify the money. If the money had been completely moved from the Alliance and Leicester Building Society to a third-party institution, it would be no longer possible to identify the fund. This would mean that the gift to Mr John Smith, of Blackacre Farm, would fail completely.

---

2 *White v Jones* [1995] 2 AC 207 per Lord Browne-Wilkinson:

> As a matter of contract, a solicitor owes a duty to the testator to use proper skill in the preparation and execution of the will and to act with due speed … The solicitor who accepts instructions to draw a will knows that the future economic welfare of the intended beneficiary is dependent upon his careful execution of the task. It is true that the intended beneficiary (being ignorant of the instructions) may not rely on the particular solicitor's actions. But, as I have sought to demonstrate, in the case of a duty of care flowing from a fiduciary relationship liability is not dependent upon actual reliance by … In my judgment, this is a case where such development should take place since there is a close analogy with existing categories of special relationship giving rise to a duty of care to prevent economic loss.

3 *White v Jones* [1995] 2 AC 207 per Lord Browne-Wilkinson.

An example where the wording is not precise enough might be:

> I give to Mr John Smith, of Blackacre Farm, a share of my bank account.

In this example there are no details as to the amount of the share. The gift would therefore fail. As a minimum, one must have three certainties: of subject, of object and of intention.[4] These three certainties in drafting remain as important in the twenty-first century as they did in the nineteenth century.

When we look at working within the certainty concepts and applying them to digital rights and digital property, we need to develop some relevant language. Unlike the commonly understood language relating to bank accounts and traditional financial assets, the language associated with the digital asset space can create confusion and discomfort. The key to removing the confusion and discomfort is to draft in clear, simple language. The language used should be easy for a non-specialist to understand. With this in mind, the first step is therefore to define the concepts of digital asset, digital property rights and a digital record.

When considering digital property rights, the following definition can be used:

> 'My Digital Property Rights' shall mean any and all rights and/or interests that are associated in any way with my Digital Records to which I am entitled at the time of my death which are eligible to be assigned, conveyed or otherwise vested upon my personal representative and/or executor.

The following definition of digital record may also be used:

> 'Digital Record' means an electronic record with which I am concerned in any way on any computing device (whether they be my Devices or devices used by me in connection with any of my Cloud Services) at my death, but excluding all my Digital Property Rights. For this purpose, 'electronic' is a reference to technology having electrical, digital, magnetic, wireless, optical, radiographic, telegraphic, electromagnetic or similar capabilities and 'record' means information that is inscribed on a tangible medium or that is stored in an electronic or other medium and is retrievable in any perceivable form. The expression 'my Digital Records' has a corresponding meaning.

---

4 *Knight v Knight* (1840) 49 ER 58.

In the event that the will or testamentary instrument contains references to cloud services used by the testator, as in the above clause, it would be appropriate to use the following definition:

> 'My Cloud Services' means any and all such services of any cloud service providers that were used by me during my lifetime and/or at the time of my death.

Specific records could be included (bearing in mind that these could be managed by a digital manager and not the personal representative and/or executor), such as:

> This will include part or the whole of the content of any message sent and received by me, and other digital text, music, images, videos, books and other similar media whatsoever.

For clients who have the benefit of smaller digital footprints and/or simpler digital estates, then a more encompassing definition maybe appropriate. The following may be useful:

> 'My Digital Assets' means any electronic record with which I am concerned in any way on any computing device (whether they be my Devices or devices used by me in connection with any of my Cloud Services or my accounts which are held remotely) at my death, including any and all Digital Property Rights and Digital Records that may be stored or located therein.

4.2 Appointing a digital executor or digital manager

In the event that the testator is appointing a personal representative and/or executor who may be technically challenged, the answer may be to appoint a digital executor. This allows one personal representative and/or executor to deal with matters in the digital sphere and leaves the other personal representative and/or executor to deal with non-digital matters. This division of the executor role into two spheres feels very natural for some people as each executor is playing to their strengths. An excellent clause to use for appointing a digital executor is the following:

> I appoint [*insert name and details*] as 'my Digital Executor', and authorise them to manage my Digital Records, Digital Rights and Digital Interests.

For some, the digital aspects of the estate may require management, particularly where there is ongoing revenue to be collected and management of digital interests. These may feel too burdensome or time consuming for an executor, even a digital executor, and therefore a digital manager may be appropriate. It is good practice where a digital manager is appointed to ensure that there is a clause providing for the cost incidental to the recovering, transferring and preserving of the testator's digital records. This can be achieved by adding the following to the above:

> My Digital Manager/Digital Executor is authorised to carry out all actions and incur such costs and expenses as may be reasonable for the recovery, preservation and transfer of my Digital Records.

By appointing both an executor and a digital executor, this allows the probate process to be split into two. It is important to note the definition of the digital executor's remit, which relates only to the digital property rights and digital interests. The definition is not simply *'My Digital Assets'* or *'My Digital Estate'*. Both of those phrases are lacking in precision, and the more general the phrase, the greater the likelihood of confusion of roles between the executor and the digital executor. In order to prevent confusion as to what exactly is within the remit of the digital executor, the more precise drafting is preferred. Simply put, the digital executor does not need to concern themselves with anything and everything digital, but only those matters relating to the digital rights and interests of the deceased.

If the testator wishes to appoint a digital executor to administer their digital property rights and interests, the following can be used:

> I appoint [*insert name*] ('my Digital Executor') to be my executor in respect only of my Digital Property Rights.

If the testator wishes to appoint a digital manager in the will:

> I appoint [*insert name and details*] ('my Digital Manager') to manage my Digital Records.

If the testator wishes to appoint executors to manage the traditional aspects of the estate and a digital executor in the will, the following may be used:

> I appoint [*insert name*] and [*insert name*] to be the Executors and Trustees and [*insert name*] ('my Digital Executor') to be my executor in respect only of my Digital Property Rights and Digital Interests.

4.3 Instructions from beyond the grave

In the event that the testator wishes to leave administrative directions for their executors and/or trustees, there are a number of possibilities. In terms of drafting, the following examples may be amended to relate to social media accounts, cloud storage or imagery contents. The following are examples of administrative directions that may be considered:

> I direct my Executor/Digital Executor to memorialise my Facebook account associated with the profile name [*insert*].
>
> I direct my Executor/Digital Executor to terminate my Facebook account associated with the profile name [*insert*].
>
> I direct my Executor/Digital Executor to terminate my Twitter account registered with the profile [*insert*].
>
> I direct my Executor/Digital Executor to delete my Digital Records from all my Devices and my Cloud Services PROVIDED THAT:
> (a) they shall have made copies of all imagery and videography digital records (photographs and videos) contained upon and within the said Devices and Cloud Services, and,
> (b) they shall have cause to reproduce copies of such imagery and videography files and distribute them to each of my beneficiaries [*insert names*].
>
> I direct my Executor/Digital Executor to copy and reproduce copies of all Digital Records found in the Device folders named 'Photos' and 'Gallery' AND distribute copies of all such Digital Records to each of my children.

When performing complex or specific directions, it is appropriate to be reimbursed for reasonable expenses. This is particularly true where there is a digital manager or third party who is not named as the personal representative and/or executor and would not otherwise be eligible to be reimbursed by the estate.

4.4 Draft clauses to dispose of digital rights and interests

Digital rights and interests may be gifted or disposed of in a similar way to other non-digital rights and interests. These may be framed in a number of different ways depending upon the complexity of the rights or interests to be disposed of. These examples would be suitable for an author or producer:

> Such of my literary works as are only in digital format ('my Digital Literary Works')
>
> Such of my videography works as are only in a digital format ('my Digital videography works')
>
> Such of my photography works as are only in a digital format ('my Digital photography works')

If the rights or interests relate only to a certain revenue stream, such as royalties, it is possible to make both a transfer of ownership and the payment of royalties to two separate individuals:

> The ownership of such of my literary works as are only in digital format ('my Digital Literary Works') to my son Joshua, provided always that any and all royalties, copyright payments and licensing revenue generated from my Digital Literary Works shall be paid to Mrs Susan Carr, of Alma Street, Woodlesford, Leeds, for the duration of her lifetime and such payments shall be paid not less than annually.

In the event that the testator is engaged in an online business, the following clauses would be suitable examples:

> My domain name [*insert name*]
>
> ... including: 'The business known as and operating as [*insert name*] and using the [*insert name*] cloud service ('my [*insert name*] business').
>
> Any and all rights and transferable benefits associated with my Amazon Marketplace Merchant account; insofar as I am permitted to transfer them.
>
> Any and all rights and transferable benefits associated with my PayPal Merchant account; insofar as I am permitted to transfer them.

In relation to rights relating to specific digital financial interests, these could be framed in a number of ways. Assuming that we are dealing with an outright gift, the following clauses may be appropriate:

> Any balance owing to me as at the date of my death, held pursuant to the terms of the contract between me and [*insert website URL or name, e.g. www.paypal.com*].

> The balance owing to me at the date of my death, under the terms of the contract between me and the bookmaker known as [*insert website URL*].
>
> All my bitcoin.
>
> The entire balance of the account owing to me at the date of my death, under the terms of the contract between me and [*insert website URL or name, e.g. Coinbase.com*].
>
> Any and all rights and transferable benefits associated with my [*insert name of retailer loyalty programme*] account.

If the gift is not an outright one, there are a number of ways of amending those clauses to accommodate other interests, such as life interest, as set out in the following section.

4.4.1 Gifting of specific items

Gifting of devices such as laptops, tablets or mobile phones is necessary and desirable. Grandparents may wish to give their laptop or tablet to a grandchild or minor for them to use for schoolwork, which does not mean they should be gifting to them the contents of the device. It should be remembered that electronic devices are able to store passwords, copies of documents and have memories that can be accessed. It should be discussed with the testator whether or not these devices should be gifted with the digital files intact. If the testator wants simply to gift the device, that means the folders, files, documents, usernames/passwords and images are transferred to the beneficiary with the device. It is clearly advisable to at least remove or allow time to copy such digital content, otherwise there is the possibility of abuse or misuse of information. The practitioner may find the following draft clause useful in these circumstances:

> My Executors/My Trustees: (a) shall take adequate steps to secure my electronic devices; and (b) have taken adequate control of such of my Digital Property Rights as may be associated with any digital records existing in relation to any and all such accounts and devices; and (c) shall have afforded my Digital Manager sufficient opportunity to recover, copy or duplicate such of my Digital Records as may be available on my electronic devices prior to disposing by gift.

Where the digital footprint is smaller, and there is not thought to be a need for a digital manager, the following alternative form may be appropriate:

> I give my laptop to [*insert name*] but I direct my [Digital] Executor, before distribution of this gift to transfer such of my Digital Records as represent my Digital Literary Works from such laptop to an external hard drive and give the said external hard drive to [*insert name*].

In the event that the testator or settlor simply intends to make an outright gift without duplicating any of the content, the following draft clauses could be used:

> I give my laptop to [*insert name*].

> I give my iPad to [*insert name*].

If, rather than copying the digital records from the device, the client wishes to delete the social media accounts, cloud storage accounts and other personal applications from the device, it is therefore advisable to include the following clause:

> ... but I direct my Executor, before distribution of this gift: (a) to identify such of my Digital Records as represent my Digital Literary Works/my Digital Videography Works/any and all personal Digital Record relating to my use of such computer; and (b) delete the same from the aforesaid computer/electronic device ...

The practitioner should remember that, when gifting a device, it is prudent for the personal representative and/or executor to ensure that all digital records belonging to the testator have been removed. When acting in a professional capacity as a trustee or personal representative and/or executor, the practitioner will owe a higher duty of care than a lay trustee;[5, 6] therefore, if the will or trust is silent as to the removal of the deceased's digital records, the more prudent route of deleting the files

---

5 *Bartlett v Barclays Bank & Trust Company (No 1)* [1980] 2 WLR 430.

6 Trustee Act 2000, section 1(1):

(1) Whenever the duty under this subsection applies to a trustee, he must exercise such care and skill as is reasonable in the circumstances, having regard in particular—

(a) to any special knowledge or experience that he has or holds himself out as having, and

(b) if he acts as trustee in the course of a business or profession, to any special knowledge or experience that it is reasonable to expect of a person acting in the course of that kind of business or profession.

(2) In this Act the duty under subsection (1) is called 'the duty of care'.

from the device prior to transferring the device to beneficiaries is recommended.

4.5 Powers of attorney

The lasting power of attorney concept was created under the Mental Capacity Act 2005 and brought into effect on 1 October 2007. The lasting power replaced its much narrower in scope predecessor, the enduring power of attorney. The purpose of a lasting power of attorney is to allow an individual, known as the donor, to appoint an individual, known as the attorney, to look after their own personal, financial or business affairs at a future point when the donor may find themselves lacking capacity. The standard lasting power of attorney form is published by the Office of the Public Guardian. The standard version is known as Form LP1F. Section 9 of the form states that:

- I appoint and give my attorneys authority to make decisions about my property and financial affairs, including when I cannot act for myself because I lack mental capacity, subject to the terms of this LPA and to the provisions of the Mental Capacity Act 2005

This means, subject to the provisions of the Mental Capacity Act 2005, that an unrestricted property and affairs attorney has authority to decide on any or all of the donor's digital assets, quasi-digital assets and digital rights or digital interests. The wording of Form LP1F, section 9 is sufficiently broad to not require any supplemental or additional verbiage to cover the donor's financially valuable digital assets.

Form LP1F does not, however, provide an attorney with the ability to operate or control a social media or cloud account. The legal authority permitting an attorney to operate and/or control a social media or personal cloud account would fall into standard Form LP1H, section 9, the wording of which states:

- I appoint and give my attorneys authority to make decisions about my health and welfare, when I cannot act for myself because I lack mental capacity, subject to the terms of this LPA and to the provisions of the Mental Capacity Act 2005

This means that the attorney has the authority to make decisions about whether the donor should take part in social activities or leisure. Social media and social networking accounts are clearly captured under Form LP1H. The power under Form LP1H means that the attorney could, if permitted by the relevant terms and conditions of the social networking account in question, operate the donor's social media accounts as well as allowing the attorney to access the donor's personal correspondence and papers, which would include email correspondence. Prescribed Form

LP1H, section 7 provides the donor with the opportunity to state their preferences or specific instructions about how the attorney should make decisions. It may be that in this section the donor provides detailed preferences as to how email and social media is to be dealt with. This may specify that certain accounts are closed. The attorney must, of course, be provided with information regarding type of accounts. That information will then allow the attorney to operate the accounts in the name of the donor.

4.6 Memorandum of wishes, also known as a letter of wishes

The memorandum of wishes, or letter of wishes, may have a number of uses when dealing with digital assets. While practitioners have historically used it to dispose of paraphernalia, chattels or items of personal property, such as jewellery, there is a versatility which is particularly useful in the digital asset field. It is, of course, a non-legally binding document and is often considered as a set of instructions or guidelines. The public nature of probate also means that a letter of wishes can be used to maintain confidential information which one may not wish to broadcast to the wider world.

There are several ways to draft a letter of wishes document. The drafting can be done informally by a lay person or by a professional. There are a number of basic rules: the document must be in writing; it should refer to the will or trust and be signed and dated by the settlor; and there is no requirement to have it witnessed. The letter of wishes could be quite a basic document or more complex depending on the settlor's circumstances. The following draft would be suitable for an average individual who does not have a detailed digital footprint:

> To the Executors of my Last Will and Testament dated [*insert date*]
>
> I appreciate that I cannot fetter your discretion in any way but I set out below the guidelines I would wish you to adopt in distributing my digital assets not expressly disposed of in my Last Will and Testament. Accordingly, I am making this memorandum to record whom I wish to receive the articles specifically mentioned or otherwise described below.
>
> Copies of all the digital images held on my iPhone and my Laptop at the time of my death shall be copied and distributed to each of my four children John, Jane, Bob and Arnold.
>
> My iPhone to [*insert name*] of [*insert*].
>
> My Laptop to [*insert name*] of [*insert*].

A more detailed letter of wishes could be useful in cases where a digital manager or digital executor is appointed. When a digital executor is appointed the following form would be applicable.

> To the Digital Executor of my Last Will and Testament dated [*insert date*]
> I appreciate that I cannot fetter your discretion in any way but I set out below the guidelines ...

The instructions to memorialise social media accounts, maintain cloud accounts and close other accounts could then be set out in the remainder of the document. There are obvious advantages to using this approach if confidentiality is an issue for the settlor. It is also versatile in that it can be written and re-written without having to conform to the formal requirements[7] of a will. The primary disadvantage is that one is relying on the good grace and faith of the individuals appointed as personal representative and/or executor, digital executor or digital manager to bring these actions into effect. In the event that the individuals appointed as personal representative and/or executor elect not to carry out the instructions or sentiments expressed in this manner, there is little recourse. This is one of the significant downfalls of these instruments. If such matters are set out in the last will and testament, there are significant legal safeguards as personal representatives and/or executors are trustees, and therefore subject to duties to exercise caution and skill,[8] as well as fiduciary obligations[9] including a legal duty of care.[10] Often, practitioners shy away from creating a last will and testament that is overly lengthy and complex preferring, instead, a letter of wishes or memorandum of wishes to dispose

---

7 Wills Act 1837, section 9(1) states that:

(1) No will shall be valid unless—
  (a) it is in writing, and signed by the testator, or by some other person in his presence and by his direction; and
  (b) it appears that the testator intended by his signature to give effect to the will; and
  (c) the signature is made or acknowledged by the testator in the presence of two or more witnesses present at the same time; and
  (d) each witness either—
    (i) attests and signs the will; or
    (ii) acknowledges his signature, in the presence of the testator (but not necessarily in the presence of any other witness),

but no form of attestation shall be necessary.

8 *Speight v Gaunt* (1883) 9 App Cas 1 at 19.

9 Trustee Act 1925, section 15 and Trusts of Land and Appointment of Trustees Act 1996, section 15.

10 Trustee Act 2000, section 1.

of personal chattels. Assuming that the testator's digital footprint and digital assets and/or quasi-digital assets concern only non-financial digital assets, it may feel appropriate to leave instructions to executors relating to matters such as the memorialisation of social media accounts and/or distribution and copying digital photographs in this type of written instrument.

Financially valuable digital assets, such as crypto-currency, should be disposed of in the last will and testament, or to a trust. The volatile nature of crypto-currency pricing means that in 2010 one bitcoin was worth US$0.08 and in 2021 the same token was valued at over US$50,000. The legal obligations on personal representatives and/or executors appointed under a will mean that there are greater safeguards for beneficiaries and the distribution of any financially valuable digital assets.

In the event that there are testamentary trusts established under a will or a comprehensive will, this does not exclude a letter of wishes. A letter of wishes may still be relevant for providing directions on matters such as guidance on how to deal with social media accounts and emails, or for dealing with personal non-financial digital assets such as photographs or family video files.

The following might be appropriate in the circumstances where a trust is involved, and the settlor wishes to communicate their desires to the trustees:

> I make this letter in reference to my Trust dated the [*insert date*] which confers discretionary powers on you and I appreciate that I cannot fetter your discretion or determine the way in which you exercise your powers. In the hope that this may be of help to you in exercising your discretionary powers, but without imposing any binding obligations on you or seeking to prevent you from acting as you think best in light of changing circumstances, I would ask you to have regard to my wishes expressed below.

Where a settlor's assets include crypto-currency or other digitally valuable assets, a letter of wishes may be used to identify the assets, as opposed to a client checklist. As a private document – rather than a public will proved in probate proceedings – there is considerable latitude for including the details of the settlor's digital wallet, profile and location of authentication documents or software. The document can be prepared by the testator and there is no requirement to have the document created by a legal practitioner. This means that the document can be edited and changed by the individual without the need for consultation, kept updated on a regular basis and adapted and changed to accurately reflect the testator's most recent holdings. A precedent for a letter of wishes dealing with a settlor's crypto-currency and financially valuable digital assets can be found at Appendix A3.

4.7 Letter of wishes and social media

A letter of wishes can also be useful for identifying the settlor's social media profile names and email protocols. These may change over time, and the editable nature by the client of a letter of wishes means that it can be a cohesive living document, as opposed to a will that is often more stagnant, and less likely to be updated with the same frequency. This letter of wishes approach can be used even in the event that the client has no other digital assets. Its versatility means that it can be as simplistic or as complicated as the probate practitioner sees fit.

A precedent for a letter of wishes dealing with a settlor's social media can be found at Appendix A3. In an estate where there is only one type of digital asset to consider, the precedent can be adjusted to meet those requirements.

5 Strategies for Digital Matters on Death – Considering Risks and Mitigation

> As the Great Parliamentarian Edmund Burke said, 'The only thing necessary for the triumph of evil is for good men to do nothing'.
>
> President John F Kennedy,
> Address to the Canadian Parliament,
> Ottawa, 17 May 1961

President John F Kennedy may have fallen into the trap of misquoting Edmund Burke, but the force behind his words is important when looking at the risks posed to digital assets. There are many possible ways of dealing with digital assets and there are also significant risks that can stem from ignoring the issues posed by digital assets. As with many aspects of life, a well thought out plan can fail in the execution or fail by not executing at all. The same is true when examining the issues in relation to digital assets. This chapter considers the types of approaches that can and should be made, how solicitors, law firms and legal representatives can mitigate the risks to themselves in relation to digital assets, and outlines the risks and possible mitigation methods.

5.1 The inactive approach to digital assets (aka doing nothing)

George Bernard Shaw said that, 'The perpetual holiday is a good working definition of hell'. If not hellish, there are certainly a number of negative outcomes that can stem from not taking any action in relation to digital assets. These include loss of data, financial loss, loss of personal information, theft, blackmail of friends and family and loss of sentimental information. These all stem from inactivity or ignorance which are often at the root of the inactive or doing nothing approach. By doing nothing, information and data are left without a user, and unlawfully intentioned individuals can then obtain access to that information. Once the information falls into the hands of these individuals, the information and data are exploited and misused to access multiple accounts, and further damage is done to the deceased's digital assets and/or digital presence.

5.1.1 The problems associated with dormant accounts (scams, harm and abuse)

Some people believe that, by doing nothing, the technology or platform providers will simply erase the information that they hold and the deceased's digital information will therefore be cleansed from the worldwide web as the years pass by. Although some websites and technology companies periodically examine their systems and arrange to delete unused and inactive accounts, this approach is by no means universal. It may take many months or, indeed, years before the deceased's account is actually purged in this manner or it may not happen at all.

While the account is dormant or not used there are a number of risks. The first is that the account could be hacked and the personal information used to set up an account with the stolen details. This could include sensitive personal information such as an individual's date of birth, mother's maiden name, address and telephone numbers. This type of personal information is not only useful to those who are criminally minded, but it also has a financial value. There are many places both on the world wide web and on the dark web where not only personal information can be sold, but also hacked accounts. So while the hacker may not convert or use the deceased's account for their own gains, they can sell the information to third parties who may use the data for illicit or criminal gain. There are a number of ways that doing nothing can cause problems for the deceased aside from the financial value of the hacked data. A dormant account is a valuable commodity to criminals as it can be used to promote phishing apps, phishing or spoofing emails, phishing websites and spoof websites to friends, colleagues and acquaintances. Those in the deceased's extended circle may not know of the deceased's death and may unsuspectingly open messages, emails or other communications from the deceased, which then introduce malicious software and/or data tracking software to their devices.

In 2021, there was a marked increase in scams of this type, which target accounts and then use the personal contacts within those accounts to introduce a fraudulent scam. For example, one scam started with a text message or email stating that 'I wanted to let you know about how I made X'. The scammer gave the name of a website where big money could be made from just a small investment. The recipient was asked to register for an 'account' and make a small deposit. This was then escalated, with further requests for money and – as an incentive – details of an increase in the value of their bogus account via a website created by the scammer for the purpose of the scam. When the recipient asked for the profits to be paid out, the fraud became apparent. This type of scam succeeds because of the credibility given to it by the initial email from a trusted friend or acquaintance.

5.1.2 Spoofing

In addition to scamming and potentially exposing friends and acquaintances to potential fraud, there is also a risk of spoofing. Spoofing – or, technically, cyber spoofing – is one of the most common types of cyber crimes. The criminal effectively imitates the deceased and uses this deception to extract the personal information or sensitive data from the other communicant and then misuses that data in an unlawful manner. By leaving the deceased's accounts open, unrestricted and unmonitored, the cyber criminal can pretend to be the deceased across multiple platforms which, in turn, makes the spoofing more convincing to the victim. Many platforms are able to take swift action on this type of cyber attack, but it relies upon them being promptly notified – often by the account user who is being spoofed. If the account is unmonitored because the user has died, this can cause significant issues.

5.1.3 The risk of becoming a gateway

There is also a risk to the deceased's own devices where they act as a gateway to a private network such as a home or office network. With the growing expansion of the smart home – or the 'internet of things', as it is also known – there are more opportunities for a cyber criminal to cause significant damage. This means that by using a hacked account, the criminal can access a device such as a mobile phone and then access the home network, which might also allow them to monitor the deceased's home security cameras, possibly causing the deceased's property to be more vulnerable to more traditional crimes such as burglary or thefts. This type of loss could clearly be significant, and this type of scenario shows how vulnerable technology can make people.

As we can see, there are significant risks to the deceased's friends, family and acquaintances by doing nothing. It can cause both financial and non-financial damage to third parties, as well as causing reputational harm to the deceased's image and standing in the community.

However, the doing nothing approach might be acceptable in some cases. For example, there is no duty or requirement on the personal representative and/or executor to do exhaustive amounts of work themselves in relation to trying to track and locate the deceased's digital accounts. Such work can be delegated to suitably qualified individuals or done by someone such as a solicitor or probate professional engaged to deal with the affairs of the estate. Best practice is to ensure that detailed records are kept as to the date that each account was dealt with. As with other communications during the probate process, it is important to document the process. This level of diligence will ensure that beneficiaries can be reassured that all reasonable steps have been taken to preserve the integrity of the deceased's personal data and digital affairs.

5.1.4 Summary

It is important to note that while this doing nothing approach may be appropriate in a very small number of cases, there will be times when it is not the appropriate approach. There is a fine line between turning a blind eye to obvious digital pathways and deciding not to expend further energies and efforts on pursuing digital pathways and possible accounts.

It is worth noting that the court will be asked to apply a common law objective test which focuses on what a reasonably prudent trustee would have done in the circumstances.[1] This reasonably prudent trustee might have done something, but they do not have to spend an exhaustive amount of time, money and energy to do it.

5.2 The active approach to digital assets (aka doing something)

Lay executors and trustees will realise that there are several ways of dealing with the deceased's digital estate. One way is to delegate to a solicitor or legal professional. The obvious question then becomes what or, indeed, how much is delegated from the lay executors or trustees to third parties, and to whom should it be delegated. Trustees and executors are not required to do all the work themselves and it is a matter of long-standing legal principle that trustees may appoint and delegate works to

---

1 *Wight and Others v Olswang (No 2)* [2000] WTLR 783.

agents,[2] providing that those agents are not also beneficiaries[3] as doing so would be a breach of the trustee's duties.[4]

5.2.1 Prohibition on delegation of trustees' or executors' powers to beneficiaries

The general prohibition on appointing beneficiaries as agents under Trustee Act 2000, section 12 should be noted by lay executors and lay trustees. In the realm of digital assets it is sometimes too simple to allow a close family member to assist in the closing down of online accounts and transferring digital documents, images and videos from one device to another. As St Bernard of Clairvaux is attributed as saying, 'Hell is full of good wishes and good intentions',[5] and it is particularly easy for the well-intentioned lay executor to fall into this trap.

Various matters should be noted with regard to delegation of powers. First, that the powers referred to in the Trustee Act 2000 must be ones which the trustee or executor had in the first place. One cannot give something that one did not have in the first place. Using social media as an example, Facebook allows users to transfer responsibility for their account on death to two legacy contacts. In this type of arrangement, the personal representative and/or executor or trustee have no power to intervene in that relationship as it is governed by the social media platform's user agreement. The user agreement is a contractual agreement and, providing the user elects to use the legacy or contact tool, the personal representative and/or executor have no *locus standi* in that

---

2 Trustee Act 2000, section 11(1) states that:

(1) Subject to the provisions of this Part, the trustees of a trust may authorise any person to exercise any or all of their delegable functions as their agent.

3 Trustee Act 2000, section 12 defines which persons that the trustees may appoint to act as agents:

(1) Subject to subsection (2), the persons whom the trustees may under section 11 authorise to exercise functions as their agent include one or more of their number.

(2) The trustees may not authorise two (or more) persons to exercise the same function unless they are to exercise the function jointly.

(3) The trustees may not under section 11 authorise a beneficiary to exercise any function as their agent (even if the beneficiary is also a trustee).

(4) The trustees may under section 11 authorise a person to exercise functions as their agent even though he is also appointed to act as their nominee or custodian (whether under section 16, 17 or 18 or any other power).

4 Trustees Act 2000, section 12(3).

5 'L'enfer est plein de bonnes volontés ou désirs', Christine Ammer, *The American Heritage Dictionary of Idioms* (Houghton Mifflin Harcourt Publishing, 1997).

arrangement. It is therefore a matter for the legacy contacts to deal with the deceased's Facebook page, Facebook images, videos and profile. This would not be a delegation of power as prohibited by Trustee Act 2000, section 12(3), as the trustees were never empowered to act regarding the Facebook page due to the pre-death arrangements made by the deceased. This example shows the power of using online tools such as legacy contact and memorialisation, as well as conducting some elemental planning on social media.

5.2.2 The standard of work done by agents or delegates

It is important to consider the standard of work to be expected of a delegated individual or agent. There is a requirement for the delegee to perform the work with reasonable care and skill. It therefore stands to reason that when the work is delegated to agents such as IT or computing professionals, they should be suitably qualified to undertake the work. There may be the desire by a probate professional when acting as trustee to undertake as much of the work as possible. It is certainly possible to obtain software that will erase data or restore a device to its factory settings and these actions do not need to be undertaken by a computing professional. However, there are times when a computing or software professional may be convenient in terms of both saving time and expense. Engaging a computer or software professional may also be appropriate where there is a significant amount of data to download, duplicate and distribute, such as a number of digital photos or images to copy and distribute to family members. There are several bodies which accredit IT and software professionals, including the BCS, The Chartered Institute for IT and The Data Management Association (DAMA UK). These bodies offer accreditation and professional qualifications for individuals engaged in the IT industry, and can act as a guide to the lay and professional executor alike when considering the type and scope of work to be covered.

5.3 Personal representatives' and/or executors' and trustees' role

There is a duty upon a trustee to act in the best interests of the estate, which is encapsulated both in common law[6] and statute.[7] Trustee Act 2000, section 1 states:

---

6 *Learoyd v Whiteley* (1887) 12 AC 747.

7 Trustee Act 2000, section 1.

(1) Whenever the duty under this subsection applies to a trustee, he must exercise such care and skill as is reasonable in the circumstances, having regard in particular—

(a) to any special knowledge or experience that he has or holds himself out as having, and

(b) if he acts as trustee in the course of a business or profession, to any special knowledge or experience that it is reasonable to expect of a person acting in the course of that kind of business or profession.

(2) In this Act the duty under subsection (1) is called 'the duty of care'.

Lay trustees owe a duty of care to the beneficiaries to act honestly, in good faith and with integrity, and to exercise as much care in dealing with the trust's affairs as a prudent 'man of business' would use in dealing with his own private affairs, or for whom he felt morally obliged to provide.[8] This prudent man of business rule has been the long-established gold standard for trustees.

There is no blanket requirement for the personal representatives and/or executors or trustees to expend all available avenues when attempting to track and trace the deceased's digital accounts. In some cases, the answer may be that there are no accounts that need to be closed. This could be the case if the deceased is an octogenarian who does not own a mobile device. It is unlikely to be the case where the deceased is younger, but one cannot apply a blanket rule based on age alone. There will be a number of other indicators to examine in each case, but where there is a user who does not own a mobile or any other computing device, there is a significantly lower likelihood of the deceased having a myriad of online accounts.

There is also the possibility that the personal representative and/or executor may have no say over the deceased's social media account or Google account. This is because several platforms, such as Facebook, LinkedIn, Instagram and Google, allow the user to appoint a legacy manager to act as a point of contact on the account. This person or persons, as there can be more than one appointee, are known as legacy managers or legacy contacts. These legacy managers or legacy contacts are appointed by the deceased to actively control or manage their profile or account on the specific platform. In the event that a legacy manager or legacy contact is appointed, there is little the personal representative and/or executor or their solicitors can do. The user agreement between the company and its users provides for this type of successor action, and the contractual agreement provides no legal standing to the personal representative and/or executor or trustee. In the event that no legacy

8 *Learoyd v Whiteley* (1887) 12 AC 747.

contact or legacy manager is appointed prior to the death of the user, the personal representative and/or executor or trustee has a role to play. The first responsibility is to notify the platform of the user's death, which will usually require documentary evidence in the form of a death certificate or possibly the production of the obituary notice. Few will require a copy of the grant of probate, although some may request a copy of the will. While each platform is different, the general options available to personal representatives and/or executors are largely the same. The choices will be either to memorialise the account or to delete it. Memorialising an account means that it continues to exist, but there is no functionality. This means that there is no data to hack into and there is no opportunity for the cyber criminal to use the account to spoof or phish. The other alternative is deletion. Deletion will result in the erasing of the deceased's data and the closing of the account.

6 Advising the Personal Representatives and/or Executors and/or Beneficiaries

Please Sir, I want some more.

Oliver Twist, Charles Dickens

There are a number of matters that need to be communicated to the personal representatives and/or executors when they begin acting in an estate. It is highly likely that many lay people will have little or no understanding of the depth and breadth of digital assets, or how digital assets apply to an estate. It is vital that this is dealt with in language that is accessible and easily understood by the lay person. There is one recent example where the solicitor informed an executor about the licensing, propriety, security and copyright issues at length in a consultation. Following the comprehensive explanation, the executor asked, 'So are you telling me I can't sell his iPad to the second hand shop?'

6.1 Distribution matters – non-financial issues

6.1.1 Digital authorship issues such as ebooks

Fifteen years ago there would have been limited need, if any, to consider digital authorship in terms of the probate of an estate. In 2016, the Nielsen Books and Consumers UK Survey found that self-published titles made up 22% of the whole UK ebook market.[1] That growth rate has continued to balloon and as of 2018, self-published ebooks accounted for 30% of the overall ebook sales.[2] There are now estimated to be in excess of 1.4 million self-published titles on Amazon's Kindle platform, and traditional vanity

1 Lisa Campbell, 'Self-published titles "22% of UK e-book market"', *The Bookseller*, 23 March 2016, www.thebookseller.com.

2 *The Publishers Association Yearbook 2018* (The Publishers Association, 2018).

publishers – once the market dominant force in the self-publishing market – account for only about 6% of all new self-published titles. The dominant forces now are digital media platforms, such as Amazon's CreateSpace.

The question then becomes what should personal representatives and/or executors be advised about ebooks? The first issue to identify is where the self-published ebook titles are registered. In reality, this is much easier than one might think. The platforms will submit monthly or quarterly reports to self-publishing authors who are presently registered on their respective platforms. Amazon operates an extensive 'lending library' to its Kindle, and tracks usage by title. The periodic reports to the author note the individual titles and the number of times each title has been 'borrowed' on the system. Royalties in respect of each title borrowed are paid by Amazon to the author via a direct deposit (sometimes referred to as an electronic funds transfer) to the author's bank account.

Therefore, the first thing to do when looking for ebook royalty payments is to search for the periodic report or the deposits from Amazon's KDP Select Global Fund. As with all deposits to a bank account, the relevant deposit should be visible on the bank account ledger entries. For many who have been in probate and private client practice for many years it will be second nature to obtain at least 8 years of bank statements. Usually, this is for determining gifts or potentially exempt transfers for inheritance tax purposes, but it is incredibly useful when tracing payments into an account from self-publishing platforms, such Apple Books for Authors or Amazon Kindle.

Once it has been established that the ebooks are active on the respective self-publishing platform, each relevant platform will need to be notified and a decision can then be made in respect of future royalty payments and the future of the individual self-published ebook titles. For example, the decision may be made to delete the ebook titles from the platform, which may be appropriate where the royalty payments are minute and irregular, causing more of an accounting headache than anything practical. If the decision is to keep the ebook titles online, there will need to be a transfer of the ownership of the individual titles. This may be a straightforward matter, particularly where there is a sole beneficiary such as a surviving spouse, but it may be more complicated where there are multiple beneficiaries. In the event that there are multiple titles and multiple beneficiaries, the personal representatives and/or executors will have to seek guidance from the testamentary documents. In such cases, it is invariably better for the rights to be left as individual legacies or transferred into a suitable vehicle such as a trust, rather than divided between multiple residual beneficiaries.

6.2 The role of the digital executor or digital manager

In some cases, the personal representative and/or executor is not sufficiently experienced in digital matters to organise and locate the relevant information, and it may be necessary to enlist the help of a more experienced individual. The role of this individual is very often to locate and trace the digital assets. The next step is to sort and organise the data, which invariably means copying and securing the data so that it can be distributed to the beneficiaries of the estate. In some cases, it is also necessary to create a register of the digital assets which have a financial value for inheritance tax purposes, such as where the deceased's estate includes digital assets – crypto-currencies or non-fungible tokens, for example – and it is important to note their existence and deal with the tax implications.

There is a distinct difference between a digital manager and a digital executor, although the titles are sometimes used interchangeably by lay people. In the strict sense of an estate where there is no will, the personal representatives and/or executors would appoint a digital manager. That individual would need to report directly to the personal representatives and/or executors and be paid by them. The digital manager would have no authority to act without the agreement of the personal representatives and/or executors. A digital executor is named and appointed by the last will and testament of the deceased. This is an important distinction as it allows the digital executor the ability to deal with the digital matters without the direct supervision of the personal representatives and/or executors. A digital executor would be paid out of the estate expenses, whereas the digital manager would be paid by the personal representatives and/or executors, who would then be eligible for a reimbursement from the estate. The difference is a subtle one and in terms of payment it is always more preferable to be in the position of the executor, digital or otherwise, as they have first call upon the assets of the estate.

6.3 Is a digital manager necessary?

A digital manager may be appointed by the personal representatives and/or executors as part of the estate administration. This is a key difference from a digital executor who must be appointed under the terms of the deceased's will. In practice, the roles are similar in nature and involve dealing with the digital aspects of the deceased's affairs. This includes issues relating to software, hardware and cloud digital records.

It may not be appropriate in all cases to appoint a digital manager as it will add to the cost of administering the estate. A digital manager may be appropriate where there is a significant number of self-published ebooks, blogs or vlogs[3] or a significant amount of digital data to be recovered or managed. The digital manager can also compile, download and copy data, thereby freeing up personal representatives and/or executors to deal with other aspects of the estate administration. Ultimately, it is a matter of fact and degree as to whether a digital manager's skill set is required. It is likely that the decision will be made on a case-by-case basis, but that the presence of a number of the following factors might act as indicator that a digital manager is needed:

- a blog;
- a vlog;
- ebooks actively published on one or more digital platforms;
- an extensive collection of digital imagery held in multiple media types and multiple types of storage devices, such as hard drive collections and cloud locations;
- multiple cloud accounts storing a significant volume of data;
- an active presence across multiple social media platforms;
- accounts with royalties to manage;
- ownership of digital photos, videos and digital files, such as recipe books;
- the need to delete social media and notifications to social media;
- the need to remove passwords, usernames and cached data from devices.

6.4 Secure, capture, electronically scrub and cleanse devices and hard drives

The first stage of the process for the personal representative and/or executor is to secure the deceased's devices and hardware. This will include removing tablets, laptops, mobile phones, flash drives, memory sticks and computers from the deceased's home and securing them safely. As the personal representative and/or executor is responsible for the safe custody of these devices, it may also be prudent to insure these items

---

3 A vlog is a Video bLog consisting of short posts where all or the majority of the content is in video format. Examples include postings to YouTube, TikTok videos and videos on the Vimeo platform.

against loss, fire and theft. The information on these devices forms part of the estate, as does the physical device upon which the data are stored.

6.4.1 Ascertain ownership of devices

It should be noted at this point that the personal representative and/or executor is advised not to assume that all devices in the deceased's home belong to the deceased. It is important to ascertain the ownership of each device. When the devices are gathered in, they should be catalogued and identified, using a temporary marker or sticker. Devices may belong to the deceased's employer, the deceased's own company or a third party.

Computer Misuse Act 1990 (CMA 1990), section 1 states as follows:

> **Unauthorised access to computer material.**
>
> (1) A person is guilty of an offence if—
>
> (a) he causes a computer to perform any function with intent to secure access to any program or data held in any computer, or to enable any such access to be secured;
>
> (b) the access he intends to secure, or to enable to be secured, is unauthorised; and
>
> (c) he knows at the time when he causes the computer to perform the function that that is the case.

If the personal representative and/or executor becomes overzealous in the collection and securing of devices, they may fall within the ambit of the CMA 1990, and it is therefore prudent to return the devices that belong to the deceased's employer and/or third parties promptly. No attempt should be made to access information on a device that is not owned by the deceased. It should be noted that the CMA 1990 applies to all electronic devices, including laptops and mobile phones, etc. The CMA 1990 has been tested in a number of ways, but never in the context of a personal representative and/or executor accessing the deceased's devices. There is a significant amount of case law where former employees have been successfully prosecuted for accessing their former employer's systems and devices under CMA 1990, section 1. The case law also makes it clear that it is an offence to access a device owned by an employer simply to recover personal files and personal data.[4] In relation to devices owned by the deceased, since they fall into the estate there is a logical and coherent argument that the personal representative and/or executor would be the party authorised to access the deceased's devices.

---

4 *R v Pardeep Parmer*, Westminster Magistrates' Court, 4 October 2017.

6.4.2 What information is captured and why cleansing is necessary

Every device maintains a record of the websites visited and the data downloaded. This record enables the user to easily access the same sites time and time again. Device manufacturers often make it easier to store passwords on a device and also to pair up both usernames and the relevant password. In some cases, these are held in a vault which might require a further password or they may be held locally on a device such as a mobile phone or a tablet which simply requires a PIN to be entered. While we are alive this is incredibly useful; it is also something to be very mindful of once we die. Ideally, personal representatives and/or executors will already have access to the PIN or password to access the password vault. If not, a computer professional may be needed to assist unlocking the device.

The ability for passwords and usernames to be stored on a device for future use means that it is extremely important to advise personal representatives and/or executors that one of their duties is to safeguard the digital data of the deceased. This includes taking steps to secure the deceased's computers and devices, such as tablets, iPads, desktop computers, laptops and mobile phones.

Once these devices are safely secured, it may be prudent to have them accessed in a way that captures any relevant information which is not within the range of knowledge of the personal representatives and/or executors. This need not be a full forensic examination of the devices and systems, but in some cases there might be a need for that level of scrutiny.

In most cases, once that data is captured the device will need to be wiped of all the user data associated with the deceased. In relation to personal files such as photographs, video and documents, there may be decisions that need to be made in the absence of specific instructions. One of the elections may be to leave them on the specific device and provide copies of those files to the interested parties.

6.5 Rights associated with files such as digital photographs and personal videos

This is an area where a number of rights and interests can become entangled. The first issue to consider is copyright. In English law there is no requirement for an author's or original creator's copyright to be registered. There are many misconceptions about the need for an individual owner, creator or artist needing to mark their work with a copyright symbol – such as a © – and a date. Copyright is owned by the creator of the work and pursuant to the Copyright, Designs and Patents Act 1988 lasts for the lifetime of the original owner and 70 years after that date. This means that there may be significant value to an original copyright photograph or digital file. This is particularly true if the subject of the photograph is newsworthy. Amateur photographer Karen Anvil captured a photograph of the Duke and Duchess of Cambridge with the future Duke and Duchess of Sussex on their way to church on Christmas Day in 2017, and has consistently generated an annual revenue in the region of £40,000 from licensing the image.[5] While not every person has the opportunity to photograph members of the Royal Family, there may be equally original images which also have financial value from a licensing perspective.

When looking at digital imagery, it is also worth considering whether any of the digital images are 'original works' falling within the meaning of Artist's Resale Right Regulations 2006, regulation 4(1):[6]

> (1) For the purposes of these Regulations, 'work' means any work of graphic or plastic art such as a picture, a collage, a painting, a drawing, an engraving, a print, a lithograph, a sculpture, a tapestry, a ceramic, an item of glassware or a photograph.

The Artist's Resale Right Regulations 2006 were written in the context of traditional works of art, as the artwork must be of a limited production number. Artworks which are widely produced in unlimited numbers are excluded, but with the recent rise of works of digital art being produced as non-fungible tokens this falls within the definition of the 2006 Regulations. It is important to note that the 2006 Regulations apply only to resales of artworks in excess of €1,000. The fees are then based on a percentage of the sale price and are collected and distributed to the artist or their estates or heirs. There is an important digital trend which may see an increase in fees collected under the Artist's Resale Right scheme – this is in the field of digital art and non-fungible tokens. A non-fungible token is a smart contract on the blockchain, usually the ethereum blockchain, which allows individuals such as artists and digital creators to provide a limited number of pieces of digital artwork to a limited number of individuals (normally fewer than 10). The ownership of the artwork then passes to the new owners. These smart digital contracts, which are at the heart of the non-fungible token art business, can be particularly valuable, often exchanging for digital currencies worth several thousand pounds. At present, the Artist's Resale Right scheme focuses on traditional sources of art resale such as auctions, antiques dealers and art dealers, yet there is a

---

5 '"Meghan's bump" caught by amateur Norfolk photographer', BBC News, 28 December 2018, www.bbc.co.uk/news.

6 SI 2006/346.

progressive trend towards identifying resales in the digital world. The benefit of the smart contracts on the ethereum block is that they are uniquely identifiable. There are also moves by progressive internationally renowned auction houses to auction non-fungible token art.[7] It is therefore only a matter of time before the Artist's Resale Right scheme catches up with the digital trend. Consequently, it is important for a personal representative and/or executor to identify any digital works on the deceased's devices. It is highly recommended that the estate is registered with one of the Artist's Resale Right scheme providers such as the DACS.[8] Providers such as DACS will then track both domestic and international sales and send the royalties to the estate, less their collection fees.

6.6 What to do with files such as digital photographs and personal videos

The presence of digital photographs on a deceased person's device, such as a mobile phone or a cloud storage account, leads to a number of questions. The first of these questions is to whom do the photographs belong? If they are on a device owned by the deceased's employer, there is established case law which shows that it would be unlawful for the personal representatives and/or executors to access the device and remove the images.[9] The CMA 1990 prohibits unauthorised access to a computing device without the prior consent of the owner, which in the case of a device owned by an employer would be the employer. So it is imperative for the personal representatives and/or executors to establish ownership of the particular device before accessing any data. The issue of ownership may be obvious, particularly if the deceased had maintained an inventory of their digital assets which also noted their locations and identifying marks, models and serial numbers. The deceased's cloud accounts, such as Dropbox and Google's One Drive, are areas where a prudent personal representative and/or executors should look for such data in addition to the deceased's own devices.

In the event that the deceased has an inventory of their digital assets complete with instructions on their disposal, there is nothing for the personal representative and/or executor to do other than to follow those instructions. An example of a digital assets questionnaire (also known as a digital asset inventory) with instructions can be found at Appendix A2. In the event there are no explicit instructions, prudence and tact will be

---

7 Sotherby's New York held the first non-fungible art token auction in 2021.

8 DACS, 33 Old Bethnal Green Road, London E2 6AA is a non-profit specialist in the field of artist resale and artist management rights.

9 *R v Pardeep Parmer*, Westminster Magistrates' Court, 4 October 2017.

required. There may be images and videos that may be of a very personal nature and may cause distress to the beneficiaries. There may also be photos and videos that could cause reputational harm to the deceased or to living persons. Personal representatives and/or executors should note that they owe a duty to the estate, the beneficiaries as fiduciaries and third parties who may be featured in any images. Personal representatives and/or executors should be careful to not release or distribute images or videos of individuals without considering the ramifications. In some cases it may be prudent to delete potentially embarrassing photographs rather than copying all the images and distributing them to beneficiaries, thereby causing distress as to the contents.

In short, there are three choices available when looking at digital imagery or digital videography. The first is simply to delete all the files; this, however, may cause distress, particularly if there are images or videos of family, friends and/or special moments. The second is to retain all the digital imagery and videography files. Copies can then be made and distributed to the beneficiaries of the residuary estate or family members if appropriate. The third choice is to be selective in the images that are copied and circulated. In some cases, there may be no need to adopt the third choice. It is also unlikely that the first choice will always be the most common approach. As with many things in the probate practitioner's world, it is the sensitive and discreet touch that may most commonly be needed.

6.7 Digital documents – What are they and what to do with them?

Documents are nothing new. Indeed, as set out in the introduction, the Dickensian Mr Jaggers and his hard working clerk, Wemmick, spent hours poring over documents signed and sealed, often written on vellum. For almost a century or more these documents, legal and otherwise, would change little, moving from vellum to paper but still stored in solicitors' offices across the country. Our digital age has seen a shift from paper to digital storage which, in turn, has removed the need for large-scale storage of physical documents. It is just as important today to know where these documents are stored as it was in the time of Jaggers and Wemmick. The advantage, and some may say a disadvantage, of digital documents is that they no longer require substantial amounts of physical storage space. This can be a disadvantage as it means that digital documents can be overlooked or missed.

Digital documents are simply written material whose data exists on the deceased's device. These may exist in many possible formats such as Word, Microsoft Excel, PowerPoint, HTML, Notepad, Pages,

OpenDocument Format, PDF, Microsoft Access, or many other less well-known programs.

There are a number of things to consider when faced with documents. The first is whether the deceased was the owner or creator of the document or whether they were the recipient of the document. It is perfectly possible that the document may have been received in the course of the deceased's business or as an employee. In these types of situations the document may not belong to the deceased at all. If it relates to the deceased's employment, steps need to be taken to return the files and any associated material to the deceased's former employer.

The personal representatives and/or executors do not have authority to dispose of the digital material belonging to third parties without their prior consent, and such prior consent for those purposes should be obtained in writing. If the employer wishes to retain the digital material, this can be done in one of two ways: either the employer can authorise the personal representative and/or executors to download the material and then pass it to the employer or, preferably and particularly if there is a significant amount of data involved, the device may be handed into the custody of the employer. The employer can then download the relevant material and return the device to the custody of the personal representatives and/or executors. If this avenue is adopted, the personal representatives and/or executors should ensure that there is in essence a chain of custody relating to the device. This means that a record is created of every person who accesses the device. This can include a summary of the actions taken by each user.

In the event that the deceased was self-employed or worked for their own limited company, the potential for documents is immaterial. However, if the deceased ran a limited company, there may be issues relating to the ownership of documents as to whether the deceased owns the digital documents or the limited company does. In the case of a sole trader, where there is no obvious value to the document it is important to consider the usefulness of the document in the running or winding up of the sole trader's business. It may therefore be useful to retain these types of documents for heirs.

Where the deceased is self-employed working in a freelance capacity, it is possible that digital material relates to clients and may be project work for clients. This needs to be ascertained before documents are deleted or erased from the device. It is perfectly possible that such documents that exist may be local copies of digital documents that exist in a shared cloud workspace such as Google Drive, Google Workspace, Dropbox, or iCloud. If that is the case, the collaborators will be able to access the data through the shared cloud space.

In the absence of any documents belonging to third parties on the deceased's devices, the personal representative and/or executor can consider whether or not to erase the documents. The easiest way to erase all the data is to do a factory reset. This will return the device to the original state it was in when the device was new. If the personal representative and/or executor desires to copy the files first so that the digital documents may be retained and the physical device disposed of, this can be done prior to erasing the documents or using the factory reset on the device.

6.8 Digital legal documents

The remote witnessing of wills has been a significant consequence of the COVID-19 pandemic for probate practitioners.[10] Some common law practitioners may be familiar with the concept of electronic legal formalities. There are a number of agreements that can exist in electronic form without the need for a physical signature. There are also a number of common law jurisdictions which brought about electronic wills prior to the COVID-19 pandemic, including Australia, New York, New Zealand and Ontario.

The Electronic Communications Act 2000 and the Electronic Identification and Trust Services for Electronic Transactions Regulations 2016[11] set out the statutory framework for electronic signatures. The eIDAS Regulation states:[12]

> *Article 25*
>
> **Legal effects of electronic signatures**
>
> 1. An electronic signature shall not be denied legal effect and admissibility as evidence in legal proceedings solely on the grounds that it is in an electronic form or that it does not meet the requirements for qualified electronic signatures.

---

10 The Wills Act 1837 (Electronic Communications) (Amendment) (Coronavirus) Order 2020 (SI 2020/952).

11 SI 2016/696. Adopted into UK law as the Electronic Identification and Trust Services for Electronic Transactions (Amendment etc.) (EU Exit) Regulations 2019 (SI 2019/ 89) in preparation for the United Kingdom's exit from the European Union.

12 Regulation (EU) No 910/2014 of the European Parliament and of the Council of 23 July 2014 on electronic identification and trust services for electronic transactions in the internal market and repealing Directive 1999/93/EC [2014] OJ L 257/73.

2. A qualified electronic signature shall have the equivalent legal effect of a handwritten signature.

In essence, electronic signatures have the legal equivalence of a traditional handwritten signature. It is therefore important for personal representatives and/or executors to identify any such documents in the deceased's inventory of electronic documents. Since they have the validity of traditional written agreements they should be treated as such. Simply because a contract or agreement is made in electronic form does not mean it can be deleted and put to one side. Personal representatives and/or executors should consider the implications for the estate in the event that digitally executed documents are discovered within the deceased's digital estate. This might include seeking appropriate legal advice as to the contents of the documents and the rights, warranties and/or responsibilities that may burden or bind the estate.

6.9 Dealing with blogs

In the event that the deceased operated a blog, there are two considerations. The first is to whether the blog is to be wound up or continued. If the blog uses WordPress, which is the most common hosting platform, the default is for WordPress to place it into private status. This means it will not be seen in the public internet sphere. If the personal representatives and/or executors desire an alternative outcome, a grant of probate or grant of representation will be required. In the event that the deceased was not using the WordPress platform but using their own domain, known as self-hosting, the blog will remain in the public sphere. It will, however, be deleted once the hosting provider is not paid for the hosting service. This may take some time, particularly if payments are set up on an automatic renewal using the deceased's credit card or bank account, and the renewal periods could be annual or a multi-year subscription. It is therefore important for the personal representatives and/or executors to look at how any self-hosting is paid for. This should be apparent from the deceased's emails, bank statements or credit card accounts.

6.10 Distribution matters – financial issues

There may be a number of institutions that need to be contacted in relation to the deceased's digital estate. Those are considered at the appropriate chapter in this work. In terms of distribution of financial interests to beneficiaries and legatees, there needs to be consideration of whether a digital or a more traditional transfer is desirable. A traditional transfer would be along the lines of a liquidation of the financial assets and payment out of the estate to the respective beneficiary or legatee. In the digital sphere it may be possible to consider a transfer of the digital financial asset to an individual or institution, this process could look similar to a stock or share transfer.

With both institutional and individual beneficiaries and legatees, it is important to ask them how they wish to receive any legacy. This is particularly important where a legacy is specific, for example:

> To my alma mater the University of Leeds, I leave three of my bitcoin.
>
> To my nephew John Smith of Jack Lane, Hunslet, I leave the balances held in my crypto-currency digital wallet.

In both examples there is a specific digital asset which is identified in the will and there is a specific individual or institution. Traditionally, institutions and charities might prefer an outright transfer of stocks and shares from the estate to their own portfolio holdings. It is possible to do the same with digital assets, particularly in terms of crypto-currency. Probate professionals should communicate with the individuals or institutions to determine how the transfer is to be dealt with and receive written confirmation of the same. When communicating with individuals it is easy to assume that the individual would prefer a payment out option. With traditional binary assets such as bank or building society accounts volatility of price is not a factor. The volatile nature of crypto-currency is a significant factor that needs to be considered, and any values discussed with the individual heirs and beneficiaries need to be caveated with a suitable warning that this is merely the present value and that it can go up and down based on the price on the exchange.

Each and every digital wallet has its own processes and procedures which must be followed, and probate practitioners should ascertain these before discussing the possible transfer of the assets to the heirs and beneficiaries. Failure to understand and clearly articulate the process and requirements to the heirs and beneficiaries may create a cloud of confusion and generate misinterpretation and misunderstandings.

6.11 Online bank accounts, etc

Probate practitioners may recall the Death Notification Service for dealing with online bank accounts held with UK banks.[13] This is discussed at 8.1, but in summary it allows for multiple participating banks and

---

[13] www.deathnotificationservice.co.uk.

financial institutions to be notified using one service. This is a significant benefit for managing active accounts after the death of the registered user. The notification service allows both lay executors and solicitors to utilise the system. All users are required to register and the system records the notifications. The relevant member institutions then contact the notifier to proceed with the next steps. Institutions that are not members of the Death Notification Service will need to be contacted individually. Equally, each member institution will require compliance with its own forms and systems for all stages beyond the initial notification.

Whilst the Death Notification Service is a useful tool for the probate practitioner dealing with active accounts, it is of no use in tracing any of the deceased's inactive accounts. Fortunately, there is a free service where inactive accounts may be located, at the website My Lost Account.[14] All the accounts listed have been in an inactive state for a prolonged period of time, and in most cases the accounts are at least 15 years old. As a personal representative and/or executor, it is possible to register on the site and a date of death must be provided. Searches on the account should also include all previous names, such as maiden names, married names and birth names if relevant. The system will record all accounts, such as those opened by grandparents or parents for children, and it is important to search all possible variations of a deceased's name.

Searches through the My Lost Account website will not assist in locating business accounts or accounts relating to NS&I Premium Bonds. In cases of prizes through the NS&I Premium Bonds scheme a search should be made using the Prize Checker tool at www.NSandI.com.

Online bank accounts may also be located by reference to the deceased tax returns, assuming that there was interest paid during the relevant tax year. It is worth cross-checking copies of the deceased's self-assessment tax returns as accounts that once were interest-bearing may at this point be at a nil rate. This will then give a starting point for any online search.

Using these resources it is possible to build a picture of the deceased's online banking and financial accounts. It is of course possible that, even after employing these tools, some accounts may remain unlocated. One could spend many unfruitful hours contacting every single banking and financial institution in the United Kingdom, but significant consideration should be given to the lengths that one should go to when making such enquiries. In reality, there needs to be an assessment of each and every estate as to how many such enquiries should be made in each particular case. For example, it is highly unlikely that an elderly client who does not have a computer, a smart phone or tablet device would have multiple

---

14 www.mylostaccount.org.uk.

online accounts. By contrast, a 30-year-old client with numerous active online social media profiles and emails relating to online banking is likely to have a greater propensity to have online accounts.

6.12 National Savings and Investments Accounts (Premium Bonds, etc)

National Savings and Investments (NS&I) accounts is an area where many questions are asked. There has been a significant shift in recent years for NS&I products to be opened online. Individuals can also manage their accounts online. Prize drawings can still be paid by paper warrant (to all intents and purposes a cheque) to the person entitled to the prize. NS&I accounts are not in and of themselves digital assets as they can be administered offline. Notification of death can be sent to the NS&I either online, by phone or by post. The individual is entitled to use whichever they feel most comfortable with. It should also be noted that in the case of paper issued Premium bonds and passbooks, they will need to be surrendered and can be posted to the NS&I.

Another matter for personal representatives and/or executors to note is that the NS&I will require a grant of probate for all sums in excess of £5,000 and reserves the right to request a grant of probate in relation to all NS&I savings accounts. This reserved right is to protect the NS&I from potentially fraudulent claims or payments to individuals who are not entitled to the proceeds.

6.13 Gambling and Lottery accounts

There are several online platforms dedicated to gambling and gaming. Fortunately, all of these platforms have one thing in common, which is that they need a source of initial funding from either a credit card, a debit card or a bank account. These funding sources are held at traditional financial institutions, so copies of the deceased statements should be readily available to those charged with handling the probate. By obtaining statements for each of the deceased's online banking accounts, the probate practitioner is afforded a comprehensive view of all transactions. By obtaining these statements and cross-referencing any payments in and out of the account it may be possible to track the deceased's online gambling accounts. Once an online gambling account has been located, a claim can be made by the personal representatives and/or executors via the relevant bookmaker or gambling platform.

It is important to note that National Lottery accounts need special considerations. The National Lottery terms and conditions state that when an account is not accessed for 168 days and there is no active direct debit, the account will be considered dormant. Unlike dormant bank accounts where the assets may be recovered at a later date, with a dormant National Lottery account the funds will be returned to the original bank account. If the account is not open the funds will be held for 6 years before being added to the National Lottery distribution fund. It is vitally important to contact the National Lottery as soon as possible to recover any funds and prizes as the account may be playing on an automated weekly basis. The time limit to claim prize money is within 180 days from the date of the drawing. This is independent from the time limit of 168 days for the account to become dormant. Personal representatives and/or executors can make a claim to the National Lottery by following the process outlined on the National Lottery website.

6.14 Online gaming accounts

Online gaming is popular with many people. There is a well-established trade in both individual online gaming accounts and prizes or rewards associated with online gaming platforms. While the trade may be thriving, the producers of the games resist such third-party trading. The terms and conditions of World of Warcraft and similar games assert that the prizes, accounts and associated digital paraphernalia are non-transferable personal assets of the registered user and they have no value outside the game. There is no established domestic case law on this point, and therefore it is something of a grey area. Clearly, as with other such contractual arrangements, for example, an Apple Music Library, the contractual terms govern the relationship.

6.15 Online trading, buying or selling accounts

Since 1995, eBay has been allowing members of the public to buy and sell items online via its online marketplace. The considerations for buyers and sellers on death are different, but in both cases it is necessary to close the account. In the case of a seller, the account fees must be fully paid up to date and all active selling must have ended. The account will then be closed between 30 and 60 days after the notification. A copy of the death certificate may be required by eBay.

In the case of an Amazon account, a copy of the death certificate must be emailed to Amazon. Any unused gift certificates can be transferred to the deceased's beneficiaries before the account is closed. Amazon reserves the right to request a copy of the will in such cases to ensure that the nominated beneficiary is an heir of the estate.

Amazon seller accounts have a number of other procedural requirements which must be met before the account can be closed. For example, the account must remain open until 90 days have passed from the last sale. This is to ensure consumer satisfaction as part of the Amazon A-to-Z Guarantee. The 90-day window from the date of the last transaction also allows for the processing of complaints and/or refunds by Amazon. With sellers who have items in storage at Amazon distribution centres, it is very important to contact Amazon as soon as possible, as Amazon charges monthly storage fees. On the death of the seller, the account holder's items can be returned and Amazon's fees deducted from the seller's account. These items would then form part of the estate unless the deceased was operating as a limited company rather than as a sole trader, in which case the items should be classified as part of the limited company's assets.

Part 4
Post-death Issues

7 Securing the Physical Aspects of the Digital Estate

Security isn't a dirty word, Blackadder.
Crevice is a dirty word.

General Lord Melchett, *Blackadder Goes Forth*

It is not surprising that probate practitioners and/or executors need to act with all due diligence to secure the assets of the deceased. In the same way that the personal representative and/or executor would physically lock the deceased's home and garage, so should they be conscious of the need to secure the deceased's digital estate.

There are a number of different matters to consider in terms of digital security. It is helpful to consider the wholly digital risks to the deceased's estate in terms of hacking, spoofing, general malware and viral infections. For further information on those digital matters, see 5.1.4.

In order to secure the digital estate we have to consider the deceased's digital pathways, and this will ultimately mean considering the deceased's physical hardware. The hardware is a vital part of the digital estate and is often overlooked. It is the repository of information which, if it can be secured and accessed, can lead to meaningful insight into the deceased's habits and show the probate practitioner the deceased's digital pathways from beyond the grave.

7.1 Securing hardware and devices

Recommended precautions that should be taken to prevent unauthorised access to the decedent's accounts include taking physical custody of smartphones, laptops, computers and hard drives. If the practitioner does not wish to physically take these items of hardware into their custody, it is essential to restrict access. Restricting access may take one of two forms: first, the hardware may be physically locked up or otherwise secured in a property or, second, the access information may be erased from the device's history. Erasing the information means deleting usernames and passwords from the device's history. This is not a case of completely erasing the device's memory, as there may be important or valuable information contained on the hardware's internal memory. Usernames and passwords tend to be stored in a browser's history on cookies. These are a form of temporary internet file which logs the device's visit to a particular website. A suitably qualified computer technician should be able to locate and delete the files that contain any history of passwords and usernames. It should be noted that using a deceased person's computer to access their quasi-digital assets and/or online accounts could be considered an offence under the CMA 1990. There is, however, much debate upon this point because clearly in the absence of the deceased the lawful authority vests in the personal representatives and/or executors of the deceased's estate and can be delegated to their appointed agents.

One key aspect to consider when accessing or restricting access to devices is to ensure that the hardware device is, indeed, the property of the deceased. For example, if the deceased was in possession of a computer or mobile phone provided by the deceased's employer, under no circumstances should any action be taken to access the contents of the device. The only appropriate cause of action in such cases is to arrange to return the device to the deceased's employer. The deceased's employer could be requested to send any personal data from the device to the personal representatives and/or executors or their legal representatives, but under no circumstances should the device be accessed as to do so is likely to constitute an offence under the CMA 1990.

The practitioner has a professional duty to maintain client confidentiality. There is also a responsibility to safely maintain the client data. There can often be a substantial amount of data on various pieces of hardware, and the probate professional will often have to strike a balance between safeguarding and practicalities. It may also be prudent to ensure that before any devices are gifted to legacies all temporary internet files, cookies and downloaded data are purged from the device (see 6.4).

Where the deceased is cohabiting with family members, it may not be possible or practical to physically secure or lock down all the family members' devices. Equally, one should attempt to track and trace the whereabouts of the deceased's devices so that an inventory of any devices, digital accounts and digital and quasi-digital assets can be taken. The days when it was considered permissible to allow a family member to take a deceased parent's laptop or iPad after the burial service are long gone.

7.2 Information capture, cleansing and storage

It is vital that once hardware is traced and secured the next step is to access the hardware. This may be by using logins provided by the deceased in the form of access to their password vault, or by a more analogue method such as a password logbook or from instructions on the client questionnaire. It may also be advisable to hire a computer or IT professional to access the hardware device if the login is not obvious or apparent. Further steps to be followed can be found in the section relating to cleansing and treatment of devices (see 6.4).

8 Dealing with Financial Quasi-digital Assets Post-death

For the probate practitioner the quasi-digital asset class is often a source of confusion or apprehension. There are a number of reasons to be concerned. The issues relating to cyber-security, ransomware and theft are at the top of those concerns. Then there is the question of where to start this process. This chapter considers how to process this type of asset, how to deal with the client information and how to deal with the primary security concerns.

In looking at these asset types, we should first consider how we deal with the testator. Not all probate practitioners have the benefit of consulting with the testator before probating an estate; however, it is important to discuss with them the importance of informing you as to the extent of their accounts. This includes all their online accounts, their digital footprint, and any or all digital assets. Most clients will have some form of online banking; indeed, for some clients this may be the only way they deal with their primary current and savings accounts. Online bank accounts are not digital assets as they do not meet the criteria of being a standalone transferrable interest. They are more accurately described as quasi-digital assets as they share some of the characteristics of a digital asset but lack a number of key features. Notably, a quasi-digital asset cannot exist independently as it is dependent upon the rights or interest of a third party. In the case of an online bank account, it is subject to the bank's standard terms and conditions. Its contents may be transferred, but the actual account is not eligible to be transferred with the agreement of the bank.

There are a number of possible actions that can be taken when faced with digital assets. In terms of quasi-digital assets, the options are quite limited. The most common option is to close them and transfer them to an estate account.

8.1 Dealing with online bank and financial institution accounts

Thankfully for probate practitioners, the system for dealing with online bank accounts held with UK banks and financial institutions in the event of death is also moving towards a unified online notification system, known as the Death Notification Service.[1] This allows for multiple participating organisations to be notified using one service. In theory, this alleviates the need for practitioners to write multiple letters to multiple organisations. The following are the participating banks and financial institutions at the time of writing:[2]

- Bank of Scotland
- Barclaycard
- Barclays
- Birmingham Midshires
- Cahoot
- CitiBank
- Clerical Medical
- First Direct
- Halifax
- HSBC
- IDEM Servicing
- Leeds Building Society (not including Leeds Permanent Building Society accounts)
- Lloyds Bank
- M&S Bank
- Marcus by Goldman Sachs
- Marsden Building Society
- MBNA
- Moorgate Loan Servicing

---

1 www.deathnotificationservice.co.uk.

2 Practitioners can confirm online whether or not a financial institution is a participating member of the service. An up-to-date list of participating institutions can be found at www.deathnotificationservice.co.uk.

- Nationwide Building Society
- NatWest
- Paragon
- Rothesay
- Royal Bank of Scotland
- Saga Savings by Goldman Sachs (for Easy Access Saving Accounts and Fixed Rate Savers opened since 30 September 2019)
- Santander
- Scottish Widows (including Scottish Widows Bank)
- Shepherds Friendly
- St James's Place Bank
- The Mortgage Works
- UCB Home Loans Ltd

The Death Notification Service allows both lay executors and solicitors to utilise the system. All users are required to register and the system records the notifications. The relevant member institutions then contact the notifier to proceed with the next steps. Institutions that are not members of the Death Notification Service will need to be contacted individually. Equally, each member institution will require compliance with its own forms and systems for all stages beyond the initial notification.

8.2 Strategies for tracing online financial assets

Once the initial death notification has been received, whether by the Death Notification Service or the more traditional route, online access will be restricted. As with traditional bank accounts, probate practitioners should obtain copies of bank statements for all online accounts.

In the first instance it is prudent to obtain a minimum number of bank statements going back 6 years from the date of death, which serves multiple purposes. First, the statements are a source for examining the deceased's cash flow, which in turn can highlight the deceased's online payment history. Secondly, they can indicate whether or not there were any significant monetary gifts to individuals prior to death, which may be relevant for the purposes of inheritance tax. Thirdly, they may indicate the existence of other online accounts, such as those relating to crypto-currency, online trading and/or marketplace activity. A number of online accounts, such as those relating to gambling/gaming, crypto-currency digital wallets, crypto-currency exchange, foreign exchange and digital off-shore accounts, all rely upon a source of initial funding that must be sourced from either a credit card, a debit card or a bank account. These funding sources are held at traditional financial institutions, so copies of the deceased's statements should be readily available to those charged with handling the probate. By obtaining statements for each of the deceased's online banking accounts, the probate practitioner is afforded a comprehensive view of all transactions.

8.3 Looking for the digital footprint behaviour pattern

It is important to remember that while not all individuals have an extensive digital footprint, it is becoming increasingly common for individuals to have multiple accounts relating to different areas of their life. Therefore, the probate practitioner should spend some time to establish the deceased's digital behaviour and any digital footprint which may remain. Enquiries can be made of the beneficiaries and/or the deceased family members in an attempt to understand the digital exposure and any known digital behaviour pattern. However, there may be unknown accounts and steps should be taken to discover or uncover financial digital assets.

Patterns of financial transactions found on the deceased's bank statements or financial account statements are an excellent indication of a pattern of online, digital behaviour. Transfers from one online account to other online accounts may rather naturally lead to further enquiries. For example, a number of transfers into a bank account from PayPal would indicate that the deceased had an account at PayPal or was using it to buy and/or sell items online. This could in turn reveal an eBay seller account or a similar type of account, such as Etsy, or both. This discovery would then lead to the practitioner creating notifications to the merchant platform regarding the accounts on either eBay or Etsy, or both, as well as notification to PayPal. From this one example we see how an initial enquiry can lead to the discovery of three additional accounts and consequently three notifications to the online platforms.

The obvious step upon discovering indications of financial transfers from or to a third-party digital platform, such as PayPal, would be to notify that financial institution. That is also the most prudent step. A notification of the user's death will ensure that the third-party institution, such as PayPal, will ensure that the deceased's account is suspended or frozen. Once that happens, the procedure for the assets to be transferred to the estate account can commence. The probate practitioner, or notifier, will be required to comply with the third party's processes and procedures associated with those accounts. Third parties such as PayPal often require both a copy of the last will and testament of the deceased account holder, the grant of probate and identification documentation of the notifier or probate practitioner. It is, however, vital that the platforms for any and all merchant accounts are contacted. These online merchant accounts may have fees that need to be paid by the estate or have annual fees or subscriptions that need to be refunded to the estate. The payment of these types of fees and/or charges may also be apparent from a credit card statement as a recuring monthly or annual charge. Notifying the digital platform of the user's death prevents these recurring charges from being levied on an ongoing basis. For most digital platforms, the initial notification can be made by email, and some platforms will need the submission of a form message through the respective website. Whichever way the initial notification is made, there will need to be a follow up with supporting documentary evidence.

8.4 Security concerns and how to handle them

The primary security concern when dealing with online accounts of quasi-digital assets is of hacking and/or unauthorised access. Quasi-digital assets such as online bank accounts, online account access for credit cards and online shopping accounts all pose a possible risk to the account holder. Many of those online accounts store potentially sensitive personal information and credit, debit and bank account information, which may be at risk of hacking or cyber-crime. Hacking, phishing and related cyber-crime are estimated to cost the United Kingdom approximately £27 billion per annum,[3] and are the most significant threats to quasi-digital financial assets. This also mirrors similar threats to digital financial assets, where hacking alone caused losses amounting to US$445 billion annually.[4] In light of these realities, it is important to take steps to ensure that accounts are secured, thereby reducing likelihood of unauthorised access.

There are a number of steps that can be taken to reduce the exposure as much as possible. One way is for the lay client to use a wide range of passwords. These can then be updated and communicated via a memorandum of wishes, which obviously needs to be actioned prior to death. This memorandum of wishes can also include references to the accounts held by the individual. By including a complete picture of their digital life in one document, this allows for prompt and efficient

---

3 *The Cost of Cyber Crime: A Detica Report in Partnership with The Office of Cyber Security and Information Assurance in the Cabinet Office* (Cabinet Office, 2011).

4 Tom Risen, 'Study: hackers cost more than $445 billion annually', US News, 9 June 2014, www.usnews.com.

notification after death. The alternative to using a memorandum of wishes is to include an inventory of the individual's online accounts. Examples of these types of inventories can be found at Appendix A2.

One straightforward way to limit unauthorised access is to promptly notify the relevant institution or institutions, which will allow them either to close the online account or to restrict online access. Once the accounts are placed into a suspended state pending the transfer of assets to an estate account, the assets have been secured.

In the event that the deceased has not used a memorandum of wishes or otherwise recorded their usernames and passwords, they may be recoverable from their devices. A number of devices retain username or profile information including passwords for regular use. Most smartphones and tablets will, in most cases, record the profile or username even if the user has not saved the password. The password is not essential to the probate practitioner as it is not always necessary to gain access to the account. In most cases, the probate practitioner can enter into correspondence or a notification process with simply the profile or username. A cursory glance at the deceased's devices may yield a significant amount of information and help to secure the deceased's online accounts.

It may not always be possible to access the deceased's devices as they may also have access controls or protection such as a fingerprint scan, PIN or password. In these cases, it will be prudent to seek the services of a suitably qualified IT professional to gain access to the devices. Once access is gained to the devices, a thoughtful inventory should be taken of any and all the assets found on the device. A number of elementary steps should then be taken, including checking the email accounts registered to the device, checking the device's browser history, and taking an inventory of files on the hard drives. Before transferring ownership to a third party such as a beneficiary, as a minimum, the browser history and stored passwords on the device should be erased. There may also be copies of files that need to be made for distribution, such as photograph imagery. In some cases, there may be limited concerns from beneficiaries about cleaning the deceased's personal data from the deceased's devices, and it is important for the probate practitioner to set out clearly the importance of cleansing and removal of the browser history and stored passwords as a minimum.

In some cases where there are shared users of an email account, such as a spouse or significant other, there may be the opportunity to transfer ownership of the email account to the surviving party from the estate.

9 An Introduction to Crypto-currencies

> … a riddle, wrapped in a mystery, inside an enigma.
>
> Sir Winston Churchill, 1 October 1939

Probate practitioners, like many professionals, have their own lexicon littered with archaic language and peculiar spellings and, to the lay person, the probate process can seem like a foreign world. While the reader will know their personal representatives from their executors, and their rights *in rem* from their rights *in personam*, the same will not be true of that rapidly growing in popularity digital asset, the crypto-currency. Crypto-currency will strike some as being on a par with Churchill's 1939 description of the Soviet Union in the epigraph above; to others, it may strike them as less puzzling. This chapter is in no way meant to be a comprehensive guide to the entirety of the rapidly evolving crypto-currency universe. It is, however, intended to be a digestible summary of what crypto-currencies are and what they are not. The chapter also focuses on some elements that are of particular relevance to probate practice. Various references to crypto-currencies are made throughout this work and the intention is that once the reader is familiar with the concepts set out in this chapter, the probate practitioner can apply the principles set out in this work to the subject.

9.1 What is crypto-currency?

Crypto-currency is perhaps best described in an apophatic manner, namely, stating the characteristics it does not have. This allows the focus to be on its key components. Somewhat confusingly, crypto-currencies are not currencies in any legal sense. The Currency Act 1751 was passed against a backdrop of colonial administrations issuing their own letters of credit for the payment of public and private debts. This caused a number of problems such as localised inflation and depreciation against the pound sterling. The Currency Act 1751 sought to regulate the issuance of letters of credit and paper bills, restricting individuals and assemblies from issuing bills as legal tender and reserving the authority to issue bills as legal tender to the Monarch in Parliament.[1] It also required that payment be in legal tender for 'any bargains, contracts, debts, dues, or demands whatsoever'. The Currency Act 1764 further extended the right of Parliament to control currency and legal tender across all North America.[2]

The Currency and Bank Notes Act 1954[3] and the Coinage Act 1971,[4] and their consequential amendments,[5] both further defined what passes for legal tender and currency in England and Wales. Using the definitions provided by these statutory contexts, there are a number of features that legal tender and currency share. None of those features, such as it being

---

1 Currency Act 1751 (24 Geo II c 53):

> An act to regulate and restrain Paper Bills of Credit in his Majesty's Colonies or Plantations of Rhode Island and Providence Plantations, Connecticut, the Massachusets Bay, and New Hampshire, in America; and to prevent the same being legal Tenders in Payments of Money … no Paper Currency, or Bills of Credit, of any Kind or Denomination, which may be made, created or issued in any of the said Colonies or Plantations, pursuant to the Provisions herein before made in this Act, shall be a legal Tender in Payment of any private Bargains, Contracts, Debts, Dues or Demands whatsoever, within the said Colonies or Plantations, or any of them.

2 Currency Act 1764 (4 Geo. III c. 34):

> … great quantities of paper bills of credit have been created and issued in his Majesty's colonies or plantations in America, by virtue of acts, orders, resolutions, or votes of assembly, making and declaring such bills of credit to be legal tender in payment of money: and whereas such bills of credit have greatly depreciated in their value, by means whereof debts have been discharged with a much less value than was contracted for, to the great discouragement and prejudice of the trade and commerce of his Majesty's subjects, by occasioning confusion in dealings, and lessening credit in the said colonies or plantations: for remedy whereof, may it please your most excellent Majesty, that it may be enacted; and be it enacted by the King's most excellent majesty, by and with the advice and consent of the lords spiritual and temporal, and commons, in this present parliament assembled, and by the authority of the same, That from and after the first day of September, one thousand seven hundred and sixty four, no act, order, resolution, or vote of assembly, in any of his Majesty's colonies or plantations in America, shall be made, for creating or issuing any paper bills, or bills of credit of any kind or denomination whatsoever, declaring such paper bills, or bills of credit, to be legal tender in payment of any bargains, contracts, debts, dues, or demands whatsoever; and every clause or provision which shall hereafter be inserted in any act, order, resolution, or vote of assembly, contrary to this act, shall be null and void.

3 The Currency and Bank Notes Act 1954.

4 The Coinage Act 1971.

5 The Currency Act 1983.

issued by a central bank or authorised by a national government and being an authorised form for the payment of all public and private debts, is presently one of the features of crypto-currency. However, on 9 June 2021, El Salvador's government authorised bitcoin as legal tender, which means it will be accepted in El Salvador as legal payment for all private and public debts in the country as of 9 September 2021 alongside the US dollar.[6]

Currencies are usually supported by a central bank or otherwise linked or pegged to the value of a commodity, such as the value of an ounce of gold, formally known as the gold standard.[7] Currencies that are not linked to the value of gold or another currency, such as the US dollar, are known as fiat currencies. In essence, these are paper bills that are supported by the full weight, credit and purchasing power of the issuing authority. In England and Wales this is the Bank of England, in partnership with Her Majesty's Treasury. This support means that there is, in essence, a range by which the currency will fluctuate, but that ultimately the British government has the ability to intervene and support the price of the pound sterling on the international currency markets. In essence, this means there is a floor to the price of the pound sterling on the international currency exchange markets, as it would be politically unacceptable for a British government to allow the pound sterling to drop to zero *vis-à-vis* other major currencies.

Crypto-currency does not have the benefit or support of an issuing authority or central bank to support it in times of crisis. It is reminiscent of those early bills of credit issued by the eighteenth-century colonial administrators, which made grand promises but with nothing to financially support them. The reason that those early North American colonial bills of credit were made unlawful by the Currency Acts of 1751 and 1764 was because they were creating instability in the mercantile markets and were seen to be deflating the value of the pound sterling. The present situation with crypto-currency mirrors the issues seen with the early North American colonial bills of credit, which were volatile in price and subject to inflation and deflation. The difference with crypto-currency is that there is no supporting body or bank to step in and regulate the existing system. For many, this lack of regulation has been one of the

---

6 'El Salvador's government is gambling on bitcoin', *The Economist*, 16 June 2022.

7 The United Nations Monetary and Financial Conference held in Bretton Woods, New Hampshire, July 1944 (Bretton Woods Conference). The Conference established a system of international currency exchange which operated from 1945 to 1970 pegging currencies to the US dollar, which in turn was pegged to gold. See 'Launch of the Bretton Woods System', Federal Reserve History, www.federalreservehistory.org.

attractions of crypto-currency, but there has in recent years been a concerted effort to attempt to increase reporting requirements around crypto-currency so that it is no longer the 'wild west'.[8] The decentralised nature of crypto-currency means that for there to be meaningful regulation, there needs to be a common international consensus on both the form and the means.

The decentralised nature of crypto-currency is one of its key features which make it unlike any other form of currency presently in existence. In the modern era,[9] financial records are held in a bank's ledger. One of the threats to a centralised banking ledger is that it can be manipulated and changed by dishonest persons causing a loss to the bank or its customers. This may be in the form of twenty-first-century cyber criminals or old-fashioned bank fraudsters. Crypto-currency stems from the blockchain technology. This technology does not use one central ledger to record information but, instead, disperses the ledger across a wide network of computers. This means that the criminally minded individual is not able to make a change on one ledger. The dispersed nature of record keeping in this way makes the system secure. One of the questions that often arises from this is whether crypto-currency is part of the blockchain. The blockchain technology may have given birth to the crypto-currency concept, but it is not a part of it. The crypto-currency and blockchain relationship is best compared to a supermarket checkout. The blockchain is the conveyor belt of the checkout desk. Items cannot get to the cashier without travelling on top of the conveyor belt, and so the blockchain is the conveyor belt, and the crypto-currency is effectively the tin of peas on the conveyor belt travelling towards the cashier to be processed. Therefore, crypto-currency is dependent upon the diversified network of the blockchain, but is also independent of it.

9.2 What is crypto-currency used for?

Crypto-currency has two primary uses. The first is as a form of bill of exchange in contracts for goods or services The second use is as a form of speculative investment. It often strikes many individuals living in developed countries as odd that a crypto-currency would be a suitable and useful bill of exchange in a contractual sense. In countries where the currency is stable and well-regulated, such as the United Kingdom, there are few concerns about issues such as hyper-inflation or governmental currency manipulation. In countries where the national currency is less

---

8 'Let us regulate "wild west" of cryptocurrency, SEC chair urges', *The Guardian*, 3 August 2021, www.theguardian.com.

9 Historically understood to be from 1450 onwards in English history.

well-respected or less free from manipulation or government interference, the fact that crypto-currency is not regulated by a central bank or other organ of the state may be seen as a distinct advantage. It therefore has a benefit in cross-border trades and transactions. It has advantages for those employing multiple freelancers in the so-called 'gig economy' across multiple countries, as all parties can be paid in the same crypto-currency.

Crypto-currency has become almost synonymous in popular culture with highly speculative investments. This is because the tokens are relatively easy to create and distribute via the internet. Bitcoin is one of the most well-known crypto-tokens, but there are at least a dozen other such crypto-tokens that are traded, in a manner similar to commodities or stocks and shares. Just like stocks and shares or commodities, crypto-tokens are bought and sold on exchanges. These exchanges exist digitally and, unlike the London Stock Exchange or any of its traditional stock exchange counterparts, they do not close – they are open 24 hours a day. This means that the digital tokens can be bought and sold at any time. It is important for a personal representative and/or executor to understand the fluidity of these types of markets as the price can move rapidly over the course of days or weeks. If a deceased's estate includes crypto-currency, it is important for the personal representative and/or executor to understand that there is the potential for the crypto-currency price to fluctuate and, in some cases, become illiquid. The personal representative and/or executor should locate the necessary information to access the crypto-currency and then make a decision on whether or not to liquidate the crypto-tokens into pounds sterling. There are tax consequences to liquidating crypto-tokens, and consideration should be given to the purchase price paid by the deceased and the potential sale price. A detailed account should be made of crypto-currency transactions within the estate because inheritance tax, income tax or capital gains tax may apply.

9.3 How is crypto-currency stored?

Crypto-currency is created by a process known as mining. Most individuals who own crypto-currencies have not mined them. In most cases, they are purchased in the secondary market known as digital exchanges. There are a number of these exchanges, the more common ones being Coinbase, BC Bitcoin, Crypto.com, Bit2Me and Quickbitcoin.

Once the crypto-token is purchased it may then be stored in a digital wallet. This may or may not be linked to a particular digital exchange. The digital wallet itself may resemble a physical hard drive, similar to a USB flash drive or it may exist as a computer programme. It is therefore very important for personal representatives and/or executors to make a thorough search for these types of devices. In the event that the access to the digital wallet is lost, there is usually no other way to access the crypto-currency. Furthermore, the position taken by HMRC is that the loss of a digital wallet does not generate a loss for tax purposes. Its position is that the asset still exists and it is simply the password or access method that is the loss, which has a *de minimis* value. It is therefore critical that executors familiarise themselves with a testator's holdings prior to death, if possible. Conversations need not be detailed, but simply sufficient to establish whether or not a testator is trading in crypto-currency and the type of digital wallet being used – information which should be sufficient in most cases.

In the event that crypto-currency is discovered on death, it may be in a single authorisation digital wallet or in a multi-signature wallet. In a multi-signature wallet, there are at least two keys required to operate the digital wallet. This can be particularly useful if these are a pooled resource, such as assets that might be owned by a syndicate. A multi-signature wallet can be very useful as it can be established with a minimum number of signatures to access it. For example, there may be six signatures assigned to the digital wallet but only four of those assigned signatures need to be used to authorise a transaction on the multi-signature digital wallet. This type of multi-signature approach is particularly useful when considering pooled funds or syndicates, as it allows multiple persons to access the digital wallet in the absence of one individual. If could also be effectively used in a probate situation where the testator wishes to have the account accessed after death but does not wish to share their own electronic signature with the personal representatives and/or executors. The account can be established using a multi-signature protocol so that the two executors can sign in the absence of the testator using their own two unique keys.

While bitcoin may be the most famous crypto-currency, there are over 3,000 other such offerings, and new ones are being created on an ongoing basis. The most common non-bitcoin crypto-currencies include:

- binance coin;
- bitcoin cash;
- bitcoin lite;
- dogecoin;
- ethereum;
- ethereum lite;
- litecoin;
- monero;
- ripple.

9.4 How does crypto-currency work?

At a very simple level, crypto-currency is a token which is minted electronically. In the same way that the Royal Mint records the numbers and denomination of the coins it mints, crypto-tokens are also recorded. Every transaction is recorded on the ledger but, unlike the traditional bank ledger which is centralised and held in one place, the records of bitcoin and its fellow crypto-currencies are held on a decentralised ledger. This ledger is divided up amongst many decentralised computers known as a network, and each computer in this peer-to-peer network is known as a node. This network of nodes is linked together using cryptography. The information verifies the data with a date/time stamp, which verifies that the data existed at a particular point in time. This date/time stamp, together with the data which accompanies it, is then connected to other blocks of data forming a chain of information. The idea is that because each block is attached to its chronological predecessor and its chronological successor, each block reinforces the other. This allows each block to reinforce its immediate neighbouring blocks, creating a string of interlinked blocks of data which, by its nature, is resistant to manipulation or modification. The data in one time/stamp block of transaction data cannot be edited or changed without altering all the subsequent blocks of data. This makes it exceedingly difficult for the blockchain ledger to be falsified and can, therefore, reduce the risk of fraud and/or reckless or negligent manipulation. This is clearly a significant advantage over a traditional, centralised ledger.

The recording of an individual crypto-token on the blockchain is only the start of the of journey. This process is known as crypto-currency mining and creates the crypto-token. The crypto-token can be exchanged or swapped for other goods or services. It was in this manner that the world's first bitcoin transactions were conducted – the first bitcoin transaction was for the delivery of pizza to an individual. Since those early transactions, bitcoin's value has increased exponentially; each bitcoin token is exchanged on a daily basis for tens of thousands of pounds on numerous digital exchanges. Bitcoin and crypto-currencies can be used as a form of payment on a contract for goods and services. They can also be used in marketing campaigns to reward individuals, which is referred to as an 'airdrop' and is becoming more common in digital marketing. In each of these types of transactions there are tax consequences to consider, and guidance has been issued by HMRC on the taxability of exchanges of crypto-currency.

Crypto-currency thrives because its users have confidence in the perceived impregnability of the blockchain. As with any currency, confidence in the crypto-token as a method of exchange is essential. If users have no confidence in the ability of a crypto-token to be accepted, it is unlikely to succeed as a token of exchange. This acceptability on a large scale makes a meaningful impact. It also marks out the most popular crypto-currencies from their lesser known peers. For every crypto-token success story there are also thousands of coins that do not make the mainstream. It is therefore important to understand that just because one holds, receives or inherits a crypto-token does not mean it is a valuable token at the point it is received. Indeed, many crypto-tokens are or become illiquid. This means that there is no market for them and no price is quoted for them on any of the digital exchanges. These exchanges simply pair up buyers and sellers and if there are no or insufficient buyers, there may be no market to be made in that particular crypto-token. An analogous situation is trying to sell stocks or shares in a public limited company while knowing that the company is bankrupt; there would be simply nothing of value to buy. Understanding what the crypto-token is will help to understand whether the contract or agreement to exchange is one of significant value or not.

9.5 Crypto-currency – altcoins and stablecoins

The term 'altcoin' has become popular in recent years. An altcoin is a crypto-token, and simply refers to any coin or token which is not bitcoin. For example ripple, ethereum and dogecoin are all altcoins. The term 'altcoin' is a combination of the words 'alternative' and 'coin'. It would therefore be possible to see in a will a clause which stated:

> To my brother Harry, I give all my altcoins. To my Sister Sally, I give all my bitcoin.

Stablecoins are a more recent phenomena and are also a form of crypto-currency. Unlike other forms of crypto-currency which are not linked to any form of hard currency, a stablecoin is linked by an actual reserve currency such as the US dollar. In theory, this makes the stablecoin less volatile, as there is a known peg between the price of the reserve currency and the stablecoin in question. This is likely to be fertile area for regulators in the near future as stablecoins presently purport to operate effectively as a method of exchange from crypto-currency and traditional hard currencies. It is likely that there will be regulations similar to those presently operating in the foreign exchange sphere. At present, the stablecoin market is worth approximately US$113 billion, but its spread is rapidly increasing, which makes further regulation of this particular sector both desirable and timely.

A probate practitioner may therefore see reference to, or be asked to draft a will dealing with, altcoins, bitcoins and stablecoins. It would be perfectly possible to see a clause such as:

> To my brother Harry, I give all my altcoins. To my Sister Sally, I give all my bitcoin. To my wife Sarah, I give all my stablecoins.

The three gifts in the above clause can be made as each meets the requirement for certainty. In the event that the deceased did not hold one of those specific crypto-tokens on death, the gift may be worthless. If the deceased used stablecoin as the reserve currency in his crypto-currency portfolio, it is likely that the largest holding would be in stablecoins. That is one of the advantages that a stablecoin has, and individuals are presently using it as a holding position between traditional currency and altcoin or bitcoin.

9.6 Facebook and crypto-currency

Since 2017, Facebook has been working on a non-decentralised blockchain-based technology, which it has referred to as 'libra'. In 2020, an announcement was made that the name libra would be changed to 'diem'.[10] Unlike other blockchain tokens or altcoins, Facebook's proposed version was supported by an association of well-known global businesses, including PayPal, Visa, Mastercard, Lyft, Uber, Shopify, Coinbase, eBay and Booking. This association was formed in Switzerland with the express purpose of overseeing the new crypto-currency. This approach is unique in the sphere of crypto-currency because existing crypto-tokens or altcoins have emerged through organic ground-up growth. Facebook's top-down approach to the issuing of an altcoin has faced a number of regulatory questions from the Bank of England as well as European, American and Japanese banking regulatory authorities. There have been a number of high-level discussions and investigations into the issues that libra/diem's launch would create.

Facebook had provided a commitment to not launch diem without obtaining approval from US Federal regulatory authorities. There were significant privacy concerns relating to tying Facebook's social media data to monetary transfer and exchanges. Facebook's proposed solution was to have the currency and transactions managed through an independent third-party company, Novi Financial. Novi would not be able to access the user's data or personal information without the user's permission. In theory, this provided a solution to the problem. A trial of the Novi Wallet

---

10 'Facebook Libra: the inside story of how the company's cryptocurrency dream died', *The Financial Times*, 26 November 2020, www.ft.com.

Application was launched using the Paxos Dollar stablecoin.[11] However, as a commercial venture, the Novi Wallet application has been abandoned and was closed on 1 September 2022.

Facebook faced a number of challenges with diem and Novi, both technically and regulatory. From a regulatory perspective, privacy concerns, banking regulation concerns and Money Laundering Regulations all posed significant challenges to both diem and the Novi Wallet application. As a consequence of these there were challenges and concerns, and Facebook and the Diem Association decided to sell the intellectual property associated with Diem to Silvergate Bank.[12] This change is not the end of Facebook's ambitions in the crypto-currency space. The end of diem and Novi has not ended Facebook's involvement or interest in digital tokens. It has simply allowed for greater consideration to be given by Facebook's leadership to other types of tokens. Recent reporting suggests that non-fungible tokens are the area that Facebook is now targeting.[13]

From a probate practitioner's perspective, it is necessary to understand how Facebook's relationship is intended to exist in relation to non-fungible tokens. It remains to be seen if all Facebook users will have a non-fungible token wallet account, or whether it will exist independently as was the case with the Novi Wallet application. It is highly likely that if there is a new non-fungible token wallet application, it will have its own protocols independent of Facebook's legacy and memorialisation functions.

Though diem was never ultimately launched, Facebook has spent a significant amount of time, effort and energy in attempting to resolve the complex financial regulatory issues that it raised. The lessons Facebook has learned from the diem and Novi Wallet experiments mean that it is significantly closer to benefiting from a successful and profitable launch in the non-fungible token space. The benefits to Facebook are clear – if only a small percentage of its 2.89 billion users operate in its non-fungible token space, there will be significant financial rewards for the company.

---

11 'Facebook launches digital currency wallet Novi', *The Financial Times*, 19 October 2021, www.ft.com.

12 'Facebook gives up on crypto ambitions with Diem asset sale', *The Financial Times*, 26 January 2022, www.ft.com.

13 'Facebook owner Meta to push ahead with digital collectibles plan', *The Financial Times*, 6 July 2022, www.ft.com.

10 Dealing with Social Media

> *Memento mori* – remember death! These are important words. If we kept in mind that we will soon inevitably die, our lives would be completely different. If a person knows that he will die in a half hour, he certainly will not bother doing trivial, stupid, or especially, bad things during this half hour. Perhaps you have half a century before you die – what makes this different from a half hour?
>
> *The Pathway of Life: Teaching Love and Wisdom*, Leo Tolstoy, 1919

It was the Victorians who took the technology of the Industrial Revolution and applied it on a mammoth scale. Their passion for technological advances that allowed them to build wonders of the industrial world, such as the Forth Bridge, was mirrored by their approach to the subject of death; and, in true Victorian fashion, death was celebrated on a colossal scale. It is not the Victorian passion for building cemeteries or the work of the enterprising founders of the London Necropolis Railway[1] that is the subject matter of this chapter. Rather, it is the way in which social media has built on the Victorians' development and popularisation of a concept that became known as 'death photography' or death portraiture. These Victorian death portraits became more popular as the cost of portrait photography fell and the methods of photography increased, leading to the growth of a mass market. Using the latest technology of the Victorian age, photographers would take images of deceased family members, often posed in family groups with living members, to preserve the moment for prosperity. Countless images exist of parents posing with their dead babies, or children with their deceased siblings.[2] Death was an ever-present threat in the Victorian age. Diseases such as cholera, typhoid, diphtheria, scarlet fever, rubella and measles were common, and the results often fatal even with medical treatment. It is therefore perhaps

---

1 'London Necropolis Railway: Trains for the dead', Lookup London, 6 November 2017, https://lookup.london.

2 'Taken from life: The unsettling art of death photography', BBC News, 5 June 2016, www.bbc.co.uk/news.

understandable that the Victorians chose to harness the rapidly advancing technology of photography to preserve the memory of their loved ones. This technology advanced the movement known to some as *memento mori* (and which became popular with the masses), where locks of a loved one's hair would be preserved in jewellery, or plaster masks taken of the deceased person's face.

While our obsession with making advances in technology has not ceased in the last hundred or so years, we have moved beyond the strange obsession of death portraiture photography and *memento mori*. They are worth mentioning in the context of this chapter, however, as they relate to present-day social media. There is still a part of the human psyche that seeks to memorialise the lives of the deceased, and there appears to be a continuation from those death portraits and *memento mori* items into the world of social media. Social media has become a place where loved ones' memories can be kept alive and remembered. In some respects, it is little different from the Victorians capturing the image of deceased relatives in photographs. It is now simply done online.

While social media users may be continuing the long trend of memorialisation and remembrance, it will come as no surprise that social media providers have not placed a direct focus on this aspect of social media. Some may say that social media providers have been slow to consider the challenges of how to deal with the death of their users. Understandably, perhaps, each social media provider has a slightly different approach to the subject. At present, there is no streamlined or unified process, but there is commonality in the approaches used by each of those providers. This chapter looks at the most commonly used social media platforms, the choices each platform offers and the processes involved.

Each social media provider has its own processes, some of which require the lay client to take certain actions prior to death. For some providers, it is possible to retain the deceased's social media profile and appoint an individual to manage the relevant profile. For other providers, it is not possible to maintain the profile beyond death of the user, but there are particular notification procedures to follow in order for the deceased's social media profile to be deleted. Since each of the major social media providers has its own processes, each is examined in turn. As not all probate practitioners will have a detailed understanding of each platform, application or format, for completeness a summary is given of the respective social media platform in turn, so that probate practitioners are able to better inform their clients.

10.1 Why is it important to understand the options and act accordingly?

For probate practitioners, it is important to provide appropriate advice to testators in relation to social media. Clients need to understand that if instructions are not provided for the actions to be taken in relation to social media accounts, the account may become dormant. Dormant accounts can be problematic as they are susceptible to abuse by the criminally minded, such as hackers or data miners. Clients should be made aware that not having a plan in relation to their accounts can allow their accounts to be abused after their death. Examples of this potential abuse include identity theft, mimicking the deceased and using the deceased's information to exploit friends and family members. This information mining or account data capture is how family and friends can be manipulated and used in fraudulent online crimes, such as phishing or impersonation. In order to prevent this type of misuse and potential abuse of personal data and/or friends and family members, it is crucial that the client develops a plan of action in relation to their social media accounts. This plan may be formally recorded in a will, codicil or digital administration document, or informally through a statement of wishes or other informal record. Draft clauses and precedents for will clauses and digital administration documentation may be found at Appendix A1.

In general, there are two approaches to social media accounts on the death of the account's registered user. The first is to have the account deleted and the second is to have the account maintained in some way shape or form.

10.2 Deleting social media accounts

Deletion is an important step as it protects the deceased user's data and their contacts from being exposed to possible illicit criminal activity. It is therefore imperative that there is a coherent approach to social media accounts because allowing one or more accounts to become dormant or inactive risks allowing the criminal element in society to exploit it. No matter what account or accounts the testator is using, deletion on death is, and always remains, an option open to all users. However, this option needs careful consideration as there can be a vast amount of data, such as images, videos and interactions, that are kept on some social media accounts. Since most of that data is held remotely on a social media cloud-based platform, it is unlikely to exist in its entirety in another location.

Therefore, deletion may mean that all that data are lost. The lay client should understand that deletion of social media accounts will eliminate all the data in the account, including images, conversations, tags, comments and videos.

10.3 Maintaining or retaining the deceased's data in social media accounts

As previously discussed, allowing the deceased's social media account to become dormant or inactive carries the risk of it falling into the wrong hands. Most social media providers permit an account to remain open in some way, shape or form. This type of data retention allows the deceased's account to remain a visible account to other users. While each platform has its own process, the concept behind this type of post-death retention allows the digital footprint of the deceased user to remain on the platform. This means that the vast amount of data, such as images, videos and interactions, generated throughout the deceased user's lifetime is retained, but strict controls are placed around that data. These safeguards vary between each platform, but the general concept is the same – namely, to retain a digital memorial or digital memories of the deceased user. The deceased user's interactions within the platform are placed in a state of suspended animation, which is often referred to as digital memorialisation.

The lay client should understand that deletion of social media accounts will eliminate all the data in the account, including images, conversations, tags, comments and videos

The following is a breakdown of the most popular social media platforms and the detailed differing ways each platform deals with the death of an account holder.

10.4 Instagram

Instagram was founded in 2010 and is a platform that operates primarily on mobile technologies such as cellular telephones and tablet computers (which includes devices such as the iPad and Kindle). The platform allows individuals to share imagery such as photographs or short video clips with a short message and normally a hashtag. The hashtag feature allows the images to be grouped together and catalogued in an effective manner. As of 2019, Instagram was one of the most downloaded apps of the 2010s,[3]

---

[3] '10 most-downloaded apps of the 2010s: Facebook dominates the decade', CNET, 16 December 2019, www.cnet.com.

with approximately 500 million daily users of the Instagram 'Stories' application.[4] Instagram was acquired by Facebook in September 2012.

There are some similarities between the options available, but presently there is no unified approach or centralised death notification system.

10.4.1 Deletion or memorialisation

Following the death of an Instagram user, there are two options that may be pursued. The first option is to have the owner's account and the associated data deleted from the Instagram platform.

The second option is to elect for memorialisation. Memorialisation allows the account to remain on the Instagram platform, while a number of account features are deactivated. Some of the key features of a memorialised account are:

- The user profile does not appear any differently from a non-memorialised account.
- The deceased's posts, photos and videos continue to be visible to the Instagram community and the audience with whom the deceased initially shared the content.
- Memorialised accounts do not appear in the public spaces of the Instagram platform.
- No one is permitted to log onto a memorialised account even if they have the appropriate username and password credentials.

Once an account is memorialised, the photographs and video imagery content uploaded to the profile may not be changed. The comments made or shared by the deceased cannot be changed after memorialisation and neither can the current profile photo, nor the followers or people that the deceased user followed. Instagram will not allow a third party access to the user account by providing login credentials or changing the privacy settings. These may all be good reasons for an individual to prefer deletion of their account upon death as opposed to memorialisation. It is important for Instagram users to understand the limited amount of control a personal representative and/or executor may have over an Instagram account once it is memorialised. For example, the memorialised account will still receive messages from other users, but no one will be able to read them. In essence, a memorialisation on Instagram becomes a virtual headstone,

---

4 'Instagram stories just passed 500 million daily users', Yahoo!, 30 January 2019, www.yahoo.com.

frozen in time, where digital traffic can take a moment to pause and reflect.

In the fast pace of the digital world in which we live this may not be the deceased user's intention, so it must be considered carefully. The election for memorialisation is irrevocable and one's executors have no control over the actual account after the user's death. It is not simply a case of allowing one's executors to manage it in the way they 'think is best'. Memorialising the account is a decision which should not be taken lightly.

10.4.2 How to request deletion of an Instagram account

To request deletion of the deceased's account, the person requesting the deletion must demonstrate that they are either:

(a) a verified family member such as a spouse, child or parent of the deceased. This must be proved to the satisfaction of Instagram and may require an individual to present a certified copy of a birth, marriage or death certificate; or

(b) a person who holds lawful authority to act on behalf of the deceased's estate, such as a validly appointed executor, executrix, administrator, or administratrix. If this is the case, the individual must furnish to Instagram a copy of the grant of probate or the letters of administration. It is possible that Instagram may request a copy of the will in addition to a copy of the grant of probate, but this is the exception to the rule rather than the norm.

It must be stressed that this is only a request that Instagram deletes the account of the deceased. Pursuant to its terms and conditions, the decision whether or not to delete a user's account is discretionary and rests with Instagram.

10.4.3 How to memorialise an Instagram account

To request memorialisation of an Instagram account there is an electronic form which must be completed. The form can be found on the Instagram website and must be accompanied by proof of death. In this case, proof of death is a low evidential hurdle. There is no requirement to present an official copy of a death certificate, a copy of the deceased's will or a copy of the grant of probate. Instagram will accept an electronic copy of the deceased's obituary, funeral order of service or link to a newspaper online obituary, which must be provided using an electronic form which can be found on Instagram's website.

Once an account is memorialised, no changes are permitted at all. The existing posts and information are effectively frozen in time. The idea is that this creates a permanent digital presence for the deceased, capturing the Instagram content right up until the date of death. The content posted to Instagram must comply with the platform's terms of use, and Instagram reserves the right to remove content that may be deemed inappropriate. This includes content on memorialised accounts.

10.5 Pinterest

Pinterest is an image-based social media platform with 416 million monthly users.[5] Sixty per cent of its user base is female and, as of the second quarter of 2020, it was growing its user base year on year.[6] With such impressive growth and a strong focus on developing its non-US account holders, it is an established presence and a growing force in the world of social media. Interestingly for such a large social user base, Pinterest does not have a significant number of complicated options from which the registered user has to choose. Additionally, Pinterest does not at present filter its platform to purge inactive accounts. It is therefore very important that the deceased's professional adviser knows of their registered profile name in advance. This will allow the personal representatives and/or executors to communicate directly with Pinterest to arrange for deactivation of the deceased user's account.

10.5.1 How to request deletion or deactivation of a Pinterest account

The deceased's account can be deleted or deactivated in one of two ways. The first is to enter the platform by using the deceased user's username and password and then request that the account be deactivated. Pursuant to Pinterest's privacy policy, it uses a series of checks to identify its users. These include sending verification emails to the email address that is on file. This form of verification or validation check is used to identify users who are requesting deactivation of their accounts. It should not, therefore, be a surprise if a number of verifications are required when using this strategy. Once verification or validation has happened, the application can then be deleted from the deceased user's devices.

---

5 'Pinterest tops 400 million monthly active users – with Gen Z, men and Millennials driving growth', Pinterest Newsroom, 31 July 2020, https://newsroom.pinterest.com.

6 '24 Pinterest stats and facts marketers must know in 2022', Sprout Social, 24 March 2022, https://sproutsocial.com.

In the event that the deceased user's username and password is not known, there is a process to follow. This is done using a standard form which can be found on the Pinterest site under the 'contact us' tab. This can be found using a site search for 'delete a deceased person's account'. The information that one must furnish to Pinterest includes the name of the user and the email address to which their account is registered. The form also asks whether the party notifying Pinterest has access to the registered email address. In the event that the notifying party does not have access to the registered email address, there are a number of documents that must be furnished to Pinterest in digital form. These documents include the legal authority to act on behalf of the deceased. This may take the form of a grant of probate or, if it has not yet been obtained, a copy of the deceased's last will and testament. Pinterest also accepts copies of death certificates or marriage certificates which name the next of kin. In the event that a death certificate is not produced, Pinterest requires a digital copy of the printed obituary. It is good practice when dealing with Pinterest to include a digital copy of the death certificate and a digital copy of the deceased's obituary. While it is an either/or situation with those documents, experience has demonstrated that the process of deactivation and removal runs more smoothly when both documents are submitted at the initial point of contact.

Once the documents have been uploaded and the online form completed, the Pinterest team will delete the deceased user's account and with it any content that was posted on there. This is not like some of its social media peers where the account is simply maintained as a memorial to its absent deceased user. Deactivation can take several days or even weeks. This is done on Pinterest's timeline and there is no sharing of information with anyone. The privacy policy clearly states that Pinterest will not share information with third parties, and that this is a policy which is strictly enforced by Pinterest.

10.6 Facebook (including Facebook Messenger)

With 44 million UK users,[7] it is highly likely that most of the clients we encounter will have registered with Facebook. Unlike other social media formats, Facebook has a diverse age range of users. Together with its Messenger application, Facebook was the number one application downloaded in the 2010 decade, having become the world's most used

7 '10 most-downloaded apps of the 2010s: Facebook dominates the decade', CNET, 16 December 2019, www.cnet.com.

social networking service by 2009.[8] This high level of usage and penetration across generations means that it is probably the one social media platform where the professional adviser can, and will, engage the most with clients. It is therefore crucial to understand the options available to the deceased and the steps that need to be taken prior to death.

Over the last 20 years, Facebook has become a vast repository of data ranging from photographs and videos, to personalised comments and memories. It has a record of the user's family and social and business milestones and events. It has moved a long way since its early origins as an electronic form of a university class year book. These memories, whether a video, a message, a photograph or a simple exchange of comments, would appear to have little or no financial value, but research has shown that these personal memories have a high monetary value to the user, on average valued at US$17,065 per person.[9] With such a significant sentimental value at stake, it is important that advisers understand the client perspective so that they are able to guide the client through the actions that are required to deal with these assets appropriately.

Facebook offers two distinct approaches to the registered user. The first is memorialisation. This allows the user's profile to remain on the platform after their death. It is not considered an 'active account' and a number of the features are deactivated. The disabled features mean that the user's birthday reminder is not broadcast to friends, but friends will still be able to post to their wall, share memories, see photographs and look at the user's uploaded content. Facebook also disables the messages features so no one is able to send or read messages sent to the deceased user through Messenger.

10.6.1 How to delete a Facebook account

It is clearly a matter for the individual user whether or not they wish their account and all the content to be deleted, and there are two avenues to make this happen. The user should click the 'Settings' tab and make the election for deletion on death. Alternatively, they can leave a directive to their appointed legacy contact to delete the account on their death. If the user has elected deletion on death, any person may contact Facebook. Facebook does not require a death certificate to process the deletion. There is an online form to complete, which requires either attaching a

---

8 Philip Gordon, *Media Tipping Points: Analyzing and Predicting Global Events* (Blue Matrix Publications, 2012).

9 Evan Carroll, 'How much are your digital assets worth? About $35,000', The Digital Beyond, 24 July 2014, www.thedigitalbeyond.com.

copy of the obituary or including the link to an electronic obituary. A news article will also be satisfactory.

10.6.2 How to memorialise a Facebook account

To memorialise the account, the user will need to appoint a 'legacy contact'. The legacy contact has some similarities to the concept of a digital executor/administrator, but is unique to Facebook, and has no authority beyond the confines of the Facebook platform. The legacy contact effectively has the ability to manage the deceased's Facebook account after their death. Importantly, the legacy contact will not be able to remove or add friends to the deceased's Facebook account. The legacy contact will, however, be able to post comments and share and upload content to the deceased's Facebook page. The legacy contact will also be able to download the deceased user's content from Facebook. The legacy contact is also able to request that the account is removed from the platform. It is therefore important that if the deceased wishes to memorialise the account, they should make their views known fully to the legacy contact.

The legacy contact is appointed by using a Facebook form. This can be accessed from either the Facebook app or on the main site. The user should click the 'Settings' tab, followed by 'Memorialization Settings', and insert the name of the legacy contact. The legacy contact must be an existing Facebook user and will be notified by Facebook that the user has appointed them as the user's legacy contact. In the event that the user changes their mind, they can follow the same steps to remove the nominated individual and replace them with another legacy contact.

10.7 LinkedIn

LinkedIn is the world's largest professional network, providing a space for professionals to network and connect. The platform is different in many ways from its more populist cousin, Facebook, but there are also a number of similarities. The quantity of information held on LinkedIn includes email addresses, users' contact information and work history, as well as commentary, posts, videos, photos and messages. This data may not be obviously apparent to users of the 'free to use' aspects of the platform. However, LinkedIn users who utilise the subscription services of the LinkedIn Sales Navigator tool will understand the enormity of the data stored on LinkedIn and the need to see that it is safely handled. The LinkedIn Sales Navigator tool provides significant access to the user database, which can then be used in the business-to-business sales cycle or the head-hunting or recruiting business.

10.7.1 What are the options for deletion or memorialisation?

LinkedIn has an option which it calls 'In Remembrance' of a user. This is in essence LinkedIn's memorialisation option. The alternative of deletion of the account and the associated data is also an option. The considerations and ramifications of 'In Remembrance' and deletion are the same as other platforms.

10.7.2 How to delete a user profile on LinkedIn

LinkedIn, pursuant to its user agreement, operates a systematic deletion process of 'inactive' accounts. This means that an individual account will eventually be deleted after a significant period of inactivity. However, there are alternatives that would allow a user's LinkedIn profile to be deleted. The first is to delete the profile prior to death. Since this is an irreversible action it is not one to be taken lightly.

The second is to provide the username and password to a trusted third party, such as a digital administrator. The appointed individual can then log onto the account and delete the profile. It should be noted that, strictly speaking, it is a breach of the LinkedIn user agreement to share a username and password to allow a third party to access your LinkedIn profile. The penalty for permitting the third party access is termination of the account and deletion. There are risks with this approach as it allows the third party full access to the profile and the data and personal information. This level of access allows the individual logging on to act as the registered user would, for example, by reading and sending messages and communications and viewing connections.

The third alternative is to leave instructions for a personal representative and/or executor to notify LinkedIn of the death. This does not require the personal representative and/or executor to have access to the account at all. There is a form to complete which is available on the LinkedIn website. The individual notifying LinkedIn will need to provide the deceased's full name, the nature of the notifier's relationship to the deceased, the deceased's email (as registered with LinkedIn, which may be a work email address), the date of death, the name of the most recent company that the deceased worked for and a link to the obituary. Upon receiving that information, LinkedIn will take steps to remove the account from the platform.

10.7.3 How to memorialise a user profile on LinkedIn

A memorialisation on LinkedIn looks different to the memorialisation on Facebook or Instagram because the functionality of a LinkedIn profile is removed. This means that much of the data is scrubbed from the user's profile and not made available to third parties through LinkedIn's premium level accounts. The user's account is effectively locked and access completely restricted, to the extent that even a personal representative and/or executor is not permitted access. The system also removes annual notifications, such as birthdays and work anniversaries. No new contacts can be made on a first-degree contact basis with a deceased user. The user's profile remains, with a banner stating that it is 'In Remembrance of' the user. This allows the profile to remain on the platform in a suspended state. The request for memorialisation can be made by the personal representatives and/or executors of the deceased user. This makes LinkedIn somewhat unique in that the decision does not need to be made by the testator in their lifetime. It is, however, useful if the user's wishes are understood as to whether or not they wish to retain a memorialised LinkedIn profile.

The process for requesting memorialisation is done through a forms message on the LinkedIn platform. The notifying party needs to provide the following information to LinkedIn in order for the account to be memorialised:

(a) The deceased user's full name.

(b) The URL to their LinkedIn profile.

(c) The deceased user's email address.

(d) The date of the user's death.

(e) A copy of the user's death certificate.

One of the following documents also needs to be provided:

(a) A copy of the letters of administration.

(b) A copy of the grant of probate.

(c) Other court order appointing the requestor as an authorised representative for the deceased member's estate.

10.8 Snapchat

Snapchat is a social messaging application that allows users to send messages to other users. It is unlike many other social media platforms or social messaging applications in that once the message is sent it deletes itself within seconds of being viewed. Snapchat is particularly popular as it has an easy-to-use photo editor that allows users to select and edit a photographic image and then send the edited image as a message.

As the purpose of Snapchat is to send short-term messages to other Snapchat contacts, the value is markedly different from Facebook or LinkedIn, where a significant amount of user data is stored. The user agreement, which exists between Snapchat and the end user, does not permit anyone other than the registered user from accessing Snapchat even if they are in possession of the username and password. Snapchat does not offer the option to memorialise or freeze accounts upon death of the registered user. The appropriate procedure to follow is for an authorised party, such as an immediate family or a personal representative and/or executor, to contact Snapchat directly with a copy of the registered user's death certificate. In order to simplify the process, Snapchat does provide an online form, which requires the authorised party to provide the death certificate. Unlike other platforms or applications, it is not necessary to have a Snapchat account to be able to report the death. The authorised party must provide their email address and the reporting party does need to know the deceased's Snapchat username. It is therefore imperative that this information is obtained prior to death as Snapchat does not presently have a policy of deleting inactive accounts.

Deletion of a deceased user's account means that the account is removed from the platform. That means the account cannot be hacked by unauthorised third parties and used for illicit purposes such as phishing or scamming. It is therefore in the best interests of the user and their friends, family and associates that the Snapchat account is deleted rather than allowed to exist after the death of the registered user.

10.9 WhatsApp

WhatsApp Messenger is a platform that connects more than 2 billion users throughout the globe. Its purpose is to provide a simple, inexpensive and secure space for the storing and sending of messages. These messages can contain words, video or digital images. These messages can be sent from one individual to another, or from or to large groups of users. This allows for a significant amount of information to be shared from one user to another. The imagery, video or words can be stored locally on the device and/or on the WhatsApp cloud-based platform.

WhatsApp offers limited options following the death of the user. The only realistic option is deletion. The standard terms and conditions of its user agreement do not provide for a death notification page or forms message system like LinkedIn or Facebook. The process for deletion is relatively simple. First, one must locate which of the deceased user's devices is logged into WhatsApp. Using that device, the legal representative or family member logs onto the WhatsApp settings menu and selects the 'delete my account' option. Once selected, the election is irreversible and the account and data will be deleted within 90 days. The information that has been shared with other users will remain as part of their conversation logs unless they elect to erase it. There is no way of retrieving that data or unsharing imagery or information posted to conversations within WhatsApp.

10.10 Twitter

Twitter is the world's largest micro-blogging site. It limits almost all users to short messages of no more than 280 characters. These messages are known as 'Tweets' and can contain imagery and words. Tweets can be seen by other users on Twitter's site and the public at large. Twitter does not presently offer a memorialisation service, so there are two options to consider when looking at a Twitter account belonging to a deceased user. The choice is between maintaining the account or deleting the account. Twitter allows immediate family members or a 'legally authorised individual' to contact it and request deletion. There is a form to complete and this can be found on the Twitter Privacy page. A 'legally authorised individual' is identified on the privacy form simply as 'lawyer'. California-based Twitter uses the term 'lawyer' generically in its online form, so it applies to any legally qualified person who represents the interests of the estate or the interests of an incapacitated person. Upon completion of the online form, contact will be initiated by Twitter. At that time, copies of the grant of probate and/or enduring power of attorney should be supplied by email, depending upon the nature of the enquiry. Usefully, Twitter will accept an electronic copy of the deceased's death certificate and is able to deactivate the account of a deceased user on receipt of the death certificate and notification from the next of kin. This is most helpful because it can be done on receipt of the death certificate rather than waiting a significant period of time for the grant of probate to be issued. When reporting or request for deactivation is done by the next of kin or 'immediate family member', the individual concerned must provide evidence of their identity. This means providing personal information in the contact form such as name, address and date of birth, which is all subject to verification. In the follow-up email in response to the online form notification, an immediate family member must be ready to upload a proof of identity such as a passport or a driving licence should it be requested by Twitter. The data acquired by Twitter in these circumstances is used solely for the purposes of establishing the identity of the individual and their *locus standi* to be able to deal with the request to delete the deceased person's account. It is not used for any other purpose such as marketing or data mining.

Twitter is not able to allow anyone, including executors, lawyers or third parties, any access to the deceased user's actual account. The account will remain locked and Twitter will not share the login information. This inactive account status is exactly what some Twitter users wish to avoid, while for others it is exactly what they want to happen. In either event, it is important that one sets the appropriate expectation with the client.

10.11 Dating websites

While dating websites may not look and feel like the social media platforms of Facebook and Instagram, they perform a similar role to a smaller circle of paying subscribers. It is important for the purposes of the probate practitioner's work to consider them as a type of social media and to act accordingly. Where the deceased was registered with one or more dating websites or applications, it is important to contact the relevant website as soon as possible. Most of these sites are based around a monthly subscription or, in some cases, a quarterly or annual renewal. As long as the deceased's account remains active, fees will be charged to the deceased's account. It is possible with these types of websites that the subscription is not charged to a debit or credit card, but to a form of digital payment account such as Apple Pay or Google Pay. Therefore, it is important to ensure that the payment method is deactivated as the bill may continue to accrue if it is not cancelled, whether or not an individual is an active user of the dating site.

11 Mitigating the Risks to the Solicitor and/or Legal Representatives

> All that glisters is not gold – often have you heard that told.
> Many a man his life hath sold, But my outside to behold
> Gilded tombs do worms enfold.
>
> *Merchant of Venice*, William Shakespeare

There is a well-worn adage that 'one cannot sue one's solicitor for work one has not asked him (or her) to do'. Clearly, work that is set out in the solicitor's retainer and letter of engagement is work that has been agreed between the solicitor and the client. It is therefore important to set out the full extent of any work that will be done in relation to digital assets. It may be that one excludes issues such as the transfer of digital assets or that such transfers and digital assets work will be conducted by the client rather than the solicitor. This may be particularly useful if the bulk of the deceased's digital assets are social media accounts, such as Facebook, LinkedIn and Twitter, etc. Such work related to notifying those platforms can be time consuming and is designed to be accessible to 'the man [or, indeed, woman] on the Clapham omnibus',[1] rather than a legally trained legal professional.

There are times when it may be necessary for that type of work to be completed by the probate professional. This is particularly true where the solicitor or legal professional is acting as a professional executor to the estate. Professional executors are not afforded the luxury of excluding part of the estate from their work. Probate professionals acting in the capacity of executors, rather than acting for lay executors, must therefore be prepared to make detailed enquiries into the estate's digital assets, including identifying all relevant devices and any accounts linked to the deceased or disclosed by their devices. The solicitor is obviously held to a much higher standard than the lay executor as they are expected to demonstrate the degree of care and skill of an experienced legal practitioner. Consideration may need to be given to the firm's professional

1 *McQuire v Western Morning News* [1903] 2 KB 100 at 109 per Collins MR.

indemnity coverage to ensure that it includes dealing with digital assets. It may also be prudent to ensure that the firm's professional indemnity coverage includes cyber liability. This can protect the firm and its clients in the event of a cyber attack whilst dealing with a client's digital assets.

Solicitors may also wish to exclude work and, consequently, any liability for dealing with the deceased's social media accounts. The work involved in locating and dealing with social media platforms can be tedious and largely administrative in nature. It does not require any specialist skill and could be done by a lay executor, if only to save on legal costs to the estate. In the event that this approach is adopted, it should be set out clearly in the terms of the engagement between the lay executors and the probate practitioner's firm.

The professional executor, not being able to exclude part of the estate, may find themselves at a significant disadvantage, particularly where there was little or no communication from the deceased regarding their digital assets, their digital footprint or the digital pathways they used. In cases where the will is drafted by the solicitor and it provides for the firm or successor firm to act as executor, it should be done on the basis that the client completes a digital asset inventory. This is designed to give the professional trustee an educated position to start from with regard to the estate. It would also be advisable to raise such matters with the client, periodically asking for them to consider updating the form if necessary.

There is an expectation that, in both scenarios, the probate practitioner will make relevant enquiries for the purposes of completing form IHT400 and submitting it to HMRC. The ability to provide provisional estimates in box 121 of form IHT400 is most useful when dealing with an estate with digital assets. These provisional estimates may change if more assets are uncovered. It is the responsibility of the personal representative and/or executor to notify HMRC promptly of the correct figure once it is available. In the event that the deceased devices are not all accounted for or devices are missing, this should be communicated to HMRC so that it is on notice.

Solicitors and probate professionals should expressly limit their responsibility for identifying, valuing and distributing the digital assets of the deceased when winding up the estate and completing the final distribution of assets. This can be done as a note within the estate accounts or as a separate disclosure document. This type of disclosure should state that it is limited to the digital assets reasonably discovered and/or disclosed to them as part of their enquiries in the handling of the estate. This prevents the solicitor's and the firm's liability being completely open-ended. Importantly, it introduces the concept of reasonableness into the actions of the solicitor or legal representative, and therefore means that they are not required to take unreasonable steps or incur unreasonable expenses. Without such a statement, either within the estate accounts or as a distinct disclosure document, it is possible that well-concealed digital assets may not be discovered and there might be a question as to whether or not the solicitor, legal representative or firm could be held liable in negligence. In all matters, it preferable to adopt a 'belt and braces' type approach that creates clarity and does not leave the matter to the vagaries of professional indemnity insurers and professional negligence litigation.

12 The Professional Executor and Legal Representative and valuing the Digital Estate

> Take nothing on its looks; take everything on evidence. There's no better rule.
>
> Mr Jaggers in *Great Expectations*, Charles Dickens

Valuation is central to the work of the probate practitioner. Indeed, Mr Jaggers reminds us to obtain evidence of values of the items which fall within an estate. Traditional assets such as art, antiques and property are relatively familiar to probate practitioners, and consequently the process for obtaining those valuations is equally familiar. Valuation of a digital estate is clearly one of the key areas that both the professional executor and the legal representative acting for the personal representative and/or executor need to understand.

The first stage in establishing value is to secure the particular assets, and ascertain which items fall within the deceased's estate. Further information in this regard can be found at 1.1 and 1.6.

12.1 Account balances

The value of digital assets is not always straightforward. Some digital assets have a clear financial value, such as a balance in a PayPal account or in a digital wallet. Where the value is in fiat currency – either pounds sterling or US dollars – there is no need to engage a valuation. All that needs to be completed is the transfer of the asset to the estate accounts. This may involve transferring foreign currencies into pounds sterling at the appropriate exchange rate on the day of exchange. All such exchanges should be recorded both in terms of the prevailing rate of exchange for the currency and any fees and commissions paid as part of any such transaction.

12.2 Vintage devices

Devices, particularly vintage ones, may have a small residual value, a significant value or no value. The humble Commodore 64 home computer, which was widely available in the 1980s and early 1990s, has a strong following among collectors. The popular Apple brand has also seen significant prices paid for its early inventions, including the early special editions of the iPod Classic and the original iPhone. There may also be valuable hardware items which are stored with vintage devices. Items such as old Atari games from the 1970s and 1980s have become collectors' items and are now traded online for thousands of pounds. The same is also true of old or vintage gaming devices, such as the early PlayStation 2 white version. As with any antique or vintage item, condition is a significant part of any value. When older devices are part of the deceased's estate, professional valuations should be sought to ensure that the estate realises the true value of any vintage computing, gaming or hardware devices.

12.3 Hardware devices

Hardware devices – such as desktops, laptops, tablet computers, mobile telephones, standalone hard drives, USB flash drives and portable devices such as Amazon's Firestick, Dots or Google Home and Nest devices, or Apple devices such as AirPods – need to be identified, catalogued and valued. For some devices, particularly the smaller more common devices, the value may be readily available from local second-hand emporiums, high street computer shops or online auction sites. Other more uncommon items – such as server cabinets, switches, racks, extenders and network bridges – may have a considerable economic value as second-hand hardware. In the case of these types of devices, a number of valuations should be sought from specialist second-hand IT vendors. Each device will retain a significant amount of data which will need to be removed prior to disposal. If the device is to be sold to a third party at a suitable second-hand market value, there are a couple of different options. The first option is for the devices to be professionally cleaned of all the personal data relating to the deceased. The second option is to restore the device to factory settings, which will erase any data that was placed on the device after the date that it left the factory. This approach can be particularly effective with mobile phones and tablet devices. In the event that data needs to be maintained, it can be transferred to the cloud, and in the case of an iPhone, the data can be backed up to the iCloud prior to restoring it to factory settings. A similar backup can be performed for Windows and Android-based products. It is a cost-effective approach that does not require any special equipment or training. It is particularly well-suited to small estates where the cost of employing technical assistance may be prohibitive or beyond the means of the estate.

12.4 Valuing crypto-currencies and non-fungible tokens

Crypto-currencies are a particularly volatile asset in the digital asset classification and should be approached with caution. The data shows that in 2020 bitcoin had a higher price volatility than stocks and shares in 2008.[1] One of the lasting lessons from 2008 was that the falling price of an asset can lead to a rapid decline in the value of a legacy or the estate as a whole. A highly volatile asset can cause some instability in the estate account valuations, but liquidation may not be an option, particularly if it is a specific legacy to a particular legatee.

Non-fungible tokens[2] are also digital assets which can add a substantial value to an estate. The market for non-fungible tokens has become more mainstream and sales of these works of digital art have been held by the major auction houses. In some cases, the works have sold for tens of thousands of pounds in excess of their original value. Where non-fungible tokens are discovered as part of the deceased's estate, a specialist valuer should be engaged. This is because non-fungible tokens occupy a rather unique position as they are digital assets but each token is also unique. Each token therefore acts as an individual work of art as well as a token which can be traded electronically. Due to this unique difference, non-fungible tokens cannot be pooled with crypto-currency or other digital tokens for tax purposes and must be identified distinctly within the estate accounts, as one might do with an estate that has a large number of works of art.

12.5 How to account for digital assets when completing form IHT400

When completing form IHT400 (or form IHT205, depending upon the size of the estate) and submitting it to HMRC, the correct categorisation is key. The notes published by HMRC which accompany form IHT400

1 'Bitcoin's price history', Investopedia, 2 July 2022, www.investopedia.com.

2 Also known as NFTs.

make no reference to digital assets in the context of either financial digital assets or non-financial digital assets. The practicalities are that digital assets, including crypto-currencies, are neither lawful currency, as they are not legal tender, nor money, so they cannot be included in box 53. They can, however, be assets of a financial nature and have a financial value. The financial value of any financial digital assets should be placed in box 76. There is provision for the legal representative or executor to make a detailed note in the 'Additional information' section on page 16.

Box 76 is the appropriate box unless the assets belong to the deceased's business, in which case box 69 is the appropriate category. For those not familiar with box 69, it is the place to record any net interest that the deceased had in a business or partnership interest. Each business or partnership needs to be listed separately, so if the deceased was in partnerships or syndicates in relation to any digital assets, the net value of the deceased's interest in each such partnership, syndicate or business needs to be listed in box 69.

13 Crypto-currencies – Taxing Matters

> The hardest thing in the world to understand is the income tax.
>
> Albert Einstein

Financially valuable digital assets, such as crypto-currencies, can be exchanged, bartered, traded and/or transferred. The value of those transfers of ownership has attracted the attention of taxing authorities in multiple jurisdictions, including in England and Wales. This has led to much consideration and detailed reports on how to accommodate crypto-currencies within the existing taxation legislative framework administered by HM Revenue & Customs. Depending upon the circumstances, it therefore follows that the probate practitioner may find that they have to consider income tax, capital gains tax and inheritance tax as they relate to crypto-currency holdings, along with the relevant case law, particularly in the case of value added tax. This chapter explores each type of tax and the implications of each to holdings of crypto-currencies.

13.1 Value Added Tax

We turn first to the case law, which derives from the bitcoin exchanging activities of Mr Hedqvist, a Swedish national. Mr Hedqvist asked for a decision from the Swedish Revenue Law Commission to establish whether Value Added Tax (VAT) needed to be paid on the purchase and sale of crypto-currency units. This was, in turn, referred to the Fifth Chamber for consideration and examination of the meaning of goods and services under the VAT Directive,[1] Article 2(1).[2] In common with cases in the

---

1 Council Directive 2006/112/EC of 28 November 2006 on the common system of value added tax [2006] OJ L 347/1.

2 Case C-264/14 *Skatteverket v David Hedqvist* [2015] ECLI:EU:C:2015:718. The Supreme Administrative Court at para 21 referred two questions to the court:

(1) Is Article 2(1) of the VAT Directive to be interpreted as meaning that transactions in the form of what has been described as the exchange of virtual currency for traditional currency and vice versa, which is effected for consideration added by the supplier when the exchange rates are determined, constitute the supply of a service effected for consideration?

European Court of Justice, the Advocate General presented her analysis to the court of the facts and summary of the case law. The Advocate General noted that there was a clear distinction between legal tender and other means of payment, such as bitcoin. It was clear that not all forms of payment were matters of legal tender. The court agreed with the Advocate General's opinion that virtual currency has no purpose other than as a means of payment. It was the opinion of the Advocate General and the court that the exchange of crypto-currencies was a supply of a service for consideration for the purposes of the VAT Directive, but that the transaction was exempt. In considering the application of VAT Directive, Article 135(1)(d), the court considered that exempt transactions involve 'deposit and current accounts, payments, transfers, debts, cheques and other instruments'. It concluded that bitcoins were a 'contractual means of payment'.[3] There are clearly similarities between that approach and earlier authorities which considered cheques, bank drafts and currency transfers.[4] In conclusion, the court's decision meant that the exchange of crypto-currencies is exempt from the provisions of the VAT Directive.

The VAT exemption applies where the contract is for the exchange of crypto-tokens to a legal tender currency, such as into pounds sterling. VAT would apply where goods or services are being traded or exchanged and the method of payment was crypto-currency. For example, while it is possible to pay a solicitor's bill in bitcoin, VAT would still be factored in to the work done under the contract or retainer. There would simply be no additional VAT for the solicitor to convert the bitcoin into pounds sterling.

13.2 Income tax

The opinion of HM Revenue & Customs is that in common with other non-digital businesses, in order to be considered a business there must be a frequency and complexity to activity that would amount to trading.[5] In the event that this threshold is met, the business will be taxed on its trading profits, and income tax would take priority over capital gains tax. This would rely upon a number of factors and is fact-specific. It is insufficient for an individual to deem their crypto-currency activity as 'trades'; the test

(2) If so, must Article 135(1) [of that Directive] be interpreted as meaning that the abovementioned exchange transactions are tax exempt?

3 Case C-264/14 *Skatteverket v David Hedqvist* [2015] ECLI:EU:C:2015:718 at para 42.

4 Case C-461/12 *Granton Advertising BV v Inspecteur van de Belanstingdienst Haaglanden/kantoor Den Haag* [2013] EU:C:2014:1745 at paras 37 and 38.

5 HM Revenue & Customs, *Cryptoassets Manual*, at CRYPTO40000, 30 March 2021, www.gov.uk.

is whether or not the individual meets 'the badges of trade'.[6] It goes without saying that this type of commercial business activity requires some degree of organisation. In securities trading, such as stocks, shares, bonds, debentures and crypto-currencies, 'the badges of trade' that could be present can be summarised[7] as:

- the length of period of ownership;
- the frequency or number of similar transactions by the same person;
- the circumstances that were responsible for the realisation;
- commercial in motive.

There is no requirement to have expenses or sophisticated equipment, or formal qualifications in either the stock trading world or the crypto-currency trading world.

In the event that the individual satisfies the requirement of operating a trading business in crypto-currencies, it is necessary to determine the trading profits. It will fall to the deceased trader's personal representatives and/or executors and their probate practitioner to complete an income tax return. Individuals may have been filing such returns for years, and in these cases it is likely that HMRC will have made a determination that trade is commercial for the purposes of income tax.[8]

The individual who is engaged in commercial trading of crypto-currencies may be able to reduce their income tax burden by offsetting any losses from their trade against future profits.

In the event that an individual is paid by an employer in crypto-currencies and the employer is a UK-based entity, the transaction should be made using the Pay As You Earn[9] operation.[10] If the employer does not account for the full amount of income tax due from employment income, the employer must make the full payment to HMRC. The employee must then reimburse the employer for the balance of the 'amount due'. That reimbursement of the 'due amount' must be made within 90 days after the end of the tax year. In the event that the employee does not make the reimbursement payment, a further income tax and national insurance charge will apply.[11] It is important for personal representatives and/or executors to be aware of the timescale to make the reimbursement of the

---

6 *Report of the Royal Commission on the Taxation of Profits and Income* (Cmnd 9474).

7 *Akhtar Ali v HMRC* [2016] UKFTT 8 (TC).

8 Income Tax Act 2007, section 66.

9 PAYE.

10 Income Tax (Earnings and Pensions) Act 2003, section 702.

11 Income Tax (Earnings and Pensions) Act 2003, section 222.

due amount. Importantly, the legislation does not state that the payment of the 'due amount' needs to be paid in monetary form.[12] Using a strict statutory interpretation of the wording of the legislation, it is possible for the employer and the employee, or in the case of an estate the employee's personal representatives and/or executors, to agree what the consideration should be to satisfy the 'due amount'.[13] Since it needs to be at least sufficient to cover the specified due amount, which is expressed in pounds sterling by HMRC, it would be possible to reimburse the employer in crypto-currency or in multiple forms of crypto-currency providing the employer is agreeable. In the event that this approach is adopted, it is crucial to detail the type of currency, the number of units transferred, the date and time of the transaction and the equivalent sum in pounds sterling. Copies of bank statements and wallet addresses should also be retained in the event of further enquiries by HMRC. This level of record keeping is required to satisfy HMRC's record-keeping requirements.[14]

13.3 Capital gains tax

In the event that the individual has not been trading crypto-currencies on a commercial basis, it is likely capital gains tax will take precedence over income tax.

Capital gains tax applies to gains made upon disposal of the asset. This means that the tax is levied on the difference between the acquisition price and the sale price, assuming that there is a gain.

For the purposes of capital gains tax, it is important to note that an individual can be treated as disposing of an asset and realising a gain even if there was no exchange of pounds sterling, or for any material value. This means that the individual would have to pay capital gains tax, calculated in pounds sterling, on crypto-currency that they had given away to another person.[15] In the event that a disposal was made to a spouse or civil partner, or a donation made to charity, the disposal would be exempt from capital gains tax.

---

12 Income Tax (Earnings and Pensions) Act 2003, section 222.

13 Ferguson and Others v Inland Revenue [2000] UKSC SPC00266.

14 HM Revenue & Customs, *Cryptoassets Manual*, at CRYPTO10400, 30 March 2021, www.gov.uk.

15 HM Revenue & Customs, *Cryptoassets Manual*, at CRYPTO41250, 30 March 2021, www.gov.uk.

13.4 Inheritance tax

In all circumstances, crypto-currencies are considered to be property for the purposes of inheritance tax. Valuation of crypto-currency assets is no different in this regard to stocks and shares. Their valuations can be located on the relevant exchanges, and the data regarding the price of each crypto-currency asset on the date of an individual's death can be calculated using historic pricing data which is widely available online. These valuations should then be noted on the inheritance tax forms and submitted as part of the estate taxing process.

13.5 Valuing crypto-currencies for tax purposes

The majority of crypto-currencies are traded via online exchanges. These online exchanges are different from traditional stock exchanges, such as the London Stock Exchange, as they do not close. They trade 24 hours a day, 7 days per week, which means that there is no close of market price.

There is also a further complication in relation to crypto-currencies and the exchanges upon which they trade, and that is one of currency. Not all crypto-currencies can be traded or exchanged directly into pounds sterling. The most common denomination is the US dollar. In the event that the crypto-currency held by the client cannot be traded or exchanged directly into pounds sterling, there is an obligation upon the individual or the estate to report the denomination of the transaction and the equivalent amount in pounds sterling. The exchange rate and the methodology used to reach the amount in pounds sterling must be maintained by the taxpayer as further enquiries may be made by HM Revenue & Customs. The probate practitioner therefore needs to maintain these additional records, particularly if the exchange or trade is not done directly in pounds sterling.

These complications can pose a problem in terms of valuation. However, there are steps that can be taken to mitigate the impact of these risks. The probate practitioner can avoid these problems by using a rigorous process. The first step is to obtain historic valuation data from an online website or portal. The second step is to determine what time will be used during the trading session. Because the market does not close, this is not as simple as saying the closing market price. Using the same time of day for every trade or exchange is one strategy. The other strategy is to use the actual trade time and date of the transaction. The same time and date data should then be applied to the timing of the conversion into pounds sterling.

Example

Applying this methodology using a fictitious cyber-currency coin known as ABC token, the transaction would be as follows:

- Time and date of ABC token sale = 2 pm or 14:00 hours on 1 October 2020.
- Gross price received on sale of ABC token = US$100.00.
- Commission paid to exchange for trade = US$2.00.
- US dollar to pound sterling rate of exchange at 2 pm on 1 October 2020 = US$1.00 is equal to £0.71.

The equation is therefore:

- US$100.00 minus US$2.00 = US$98.00.
- 98 multiplied by 0.71 = £69.58.

Using this methodology, the total sum that is reportable to HMRC is therefore £69.58. As with all systems, the methodology should remain the same. The probate practitioner should avoid alternating between methodologies when dealing within an individual estate but is not required to use the same methodology in every single estate or administration. There may be a reason to move between methodologies when dealing with a particular estate. This is particularly true when, prior to death, the testator had already established a preference for one method over the other. The issue here is consistency. If the deceased had been selling and reporting using the time/date/price method as opposed to the average price during the day method, the probate practitioner should follow the same methodology to ensure consistency with early reporting by the individual. This is particularly important in relation to the concept of pooling crypto-currencies.

13.6 Pooling and the importance of fungibility

13.6.1 What is pooling and how does it work?

Pooling is a recognised method of simplifying the calculation for the purpose of capital gains tax.[16] This method allows assets of a similar type to be brought together and traded without the need to identify the particular individual coin or token. This collection of similar asset types forms what is known as the Section 104 pool. In reality, this means that where an individual has a number of different tokens which have been

---

[16] Taxation of Chargeable Gains Act 1992, section 104.

traded, distinct pools are made within the individual's holdings.[17] So if an individual has four types of coins, each of the individual coin types forms a separate pool, for example, 'the bitcoin pool', 'the ether pool', 'the litecoin pool' and 'the dogecoin pool'. The value of each pool increases with acquisitions to the respective pool and decreases with relevant dispositions. The pool is also able to account for the charges and costs of acquisition or disposal by attributing fees and commissions to the pool as pooled allowable costs. Obviously, the more tokens or coins that are traded from or into a pool, the higher the pooled allowable costs as every trade will attract some level of fee or commission.

Those using the pooling approach must maintain a meticulous record of both acquisitions and disposals, together with any associated expenses to be used as pooled allowable costs. This approach allows the costs to be borne by the pool as a whole rather than the individual transaction of Coin A and the subsequent sale of Coin A. Therefore, in practice, the pooling approach should limit the need for very granular detail; this means that records will only need to detail token type and number entering or departing the pool together with the relevant costs. As a method for treating taxable gains, it is very efficient and not overly complicated, providing that one has access to the acquisition and disposal data for the relevant tokens or coins.

An example of the way a pool might operate can be seen below.

Example

Tom Smith has a company called Pearl Mill Coins Limited. Pearl Mill Coins Limited purchased 200 ABC tokens for £20,000.00. Two and a half years later, Pearl Mill Coins Limited purchases a further 100 ABC tokens for £200,000.00. At this juncture, Pearl Mill Coins Limited has 300 ABC tokens in one single pool, with a total allowable cost of £220,000.00. This means that if 50 ABC tokens were sold from the pool for a total consideration of £100,000.00, the total allowable cost per ABC token would be:

- 220,000 divided by 300 = 733.33

The total allowable cost on the sale of the 50 ABC tokens would therefore be:

- 733.33 multiplied by 50 = 36,666.66

---

17 It takes its name from Taxation of Chargeable Gains Act 1992, section 104.

The calculation for the taxable capital gains from the pool in this example is:

- £100,000.00 less £36,666.66 = £63,333.34

Although the example uses the company, Pearl Mill Coins Limited, the pooling rules relating to crypto-currency pools apply equally to individuals, estates and corporations, as the underlying assets in the pool are essentially the same as any other asset. This ability to swap one asset for another identical token in the pool is known as fungibility.[18]

In the case of an estate, a capital gains liability will arise where the sale of a crypto-currency token or pool takes place as part of the administration of the estate. If the asset passes under the will as a legacy, neither the estate nor the administrators will be liable for a capital gains charge. The capital gains will be chargeable to individual legatees.

13.6.2 Fungibility

The concept of fungibility applies to all assets that are identical once pooled, so it applies to digital assets and non-digital assets in equal measure. This can be useful to the probate practitioner as it allows sales of crypto-currency from pools within an estate without having to deal with individual tax lots.

Fungibility does not apply to all digital assets, and one key digital asset to be aware of is the digital asset known as non-fungible tokens. This is because a non-fungible token by its very nature is unique. The popularity of non-fungible tokens and their unique place on the digital blockchain means they are not exchangeable in a pool with another non-fungible token. It is therefore important for the probate practitioner to understand the difference between the different types of tokens that exist in the digital realm. One simple way to identify crypto-currency from non-fungible tokens is by the type of account and how the assets are held. Tokens held in a digital wallet, such as one of the many online providers, or traded on an exchange, are fungible tokens. Tokens which are sold as a certificate of ownership at individual auctions or individual sales are non-fungible tokens. As demonstrated in 2021 by Sir Tim Berners-Lee's sale of the source code for the internet, non-fungible tokens are unique and have a

---

18 HM Revenue & Customs, *Capital Gains Manual*, at CG11820, 12 March 2016, www.gov.uk.

considerable value. In the case of Sir Tim Berners-Lee, that one non-fungible token sold for £3,900,000.[19] It is therefore important to identify fungible tokens and non-fungible tokens and account for them appropriately in terms of valuation, disposal and taxation.

---

19 'Tim Berners-Lee sells web source code NFT for $5.4m', BBC News, 21 June 2021, www.bbc.co.uk/news.

Appendices

A1 Useful Draft Clauses when Dealing with or Appointing a Digital Executor or Digital Administrator

Draft definition of digital property and/or digital assets

When considering digital property rights and/or digital assets, the following definition can be used:

> 'My Digital Property Rights' shall mean any and all rights and/or interests that are associated in any way with my Digital Records to which I am entitled at the time of my death which are eligible to be assigned, conveyed or otherwise vested upon my personal representative and/or executor.

The following definitions of digital record may also be used:

> 'Digital Record' means an electronic record with which I am concerned in any way on any computing device (whether they be my Devices or devices used by me in connection with any of my Cloud Services) at my death, but excluding all my Digital Property Rights. For this purpose, 'electronic' is a reference to technology having electrical, digital, magnetic, wireless, optical, radiographic, telegraphic, electromagnetic or similar capabilities and 'record' means information that is inscribed on a tangible medium or that is stored in an electronic or other medium and is retrievable in any perceivable form. The expression 'my Digital Records' has a corresponding meaning.

'My Cloud Services' means any and all such services of any cloud service providers that were used by me during my lifetime and/or at the time of my death.

This will include part or the whole of the content of any message sent and received by me, and other digital text, music, images, videos, books and other similar media whatsoever.

Appointing a digital executor or digital manager

I appoint [*insert name and details*] as 'my Digital Executor', and authorise them to manage my Digital Records, Digital Rights and Digital Interests.

I appoint [*insert name*] ('my Digital Executor') to be my executor in respect only of my Digital Property Rights.

I appoint [*insert name and details*] ('my Digital Manager') to manage my Digital Records.

I appoint [*insert name*] and [*insert name*] to be the Executors and Trustees and [*insert name*] ('my Digital Executor') to be my executor in respect only of my Digital Property Rights and Digital Interests.

Providing for payment of digital manager, digital executor, etc

My Digital Manager/Digital Executor is authorised to carry out all actions and incur such costs and expenses as may be reasonable for the recovery, preservation and transfer of my Digital Records.

Draft instructions to a digital executor, administrator or digital manager

I direct my Executor/Digital Executor to memorialise my Facebook account associated with the profile name[*insert*].

I direct my Executor/Digital Executor to terminate my Facebook account associated with the profile name [*insert*].

I direct my Executor/Digital Executor to terminate my Twitter account registered with the profile [*insert*].

I direct my Executor/Digital Executor to delete my Digital Records from all my Devices and my Cloud Services PROVIDED THAT:

(a) he/she shall have made copies of all imagery and videography digital records (photographs and videos) contained upon and within the said Devices and Cloud Services, and,

(b) he/she shall have cause to reproduce copies of such imagery and videography files and distribute them to each of my beneficiaries [*insert names*].

A2 An Example of a Client Questionnaire

Digital assets questionnaire[1]

The term 'digital asset' is the way that the legal community refers to your personal rights, data and sometimes information, that is kept or stored electronically. It may not be stored on any one computer but on a number of computers (known as a network) or remotely through an online 'cloud' server account. These three different storage methods may belong to you or a third party. These third parties may be the companies you transact business with (such as a retailer). Anyone who uses email, makes online purchases, sells an item online, or pays bills online has some form of digital data and possibly digital asset. Digital assets generally require a username and/or password or PIN to access and can be difficult or impossible to retrieve if someone is incapacitated or passes away. Some digital assets have a monetary value while others have sentimental value. Either way, they are often very important to the people who create them, and it is therefore important that should anything happen to you then your executors or those with powers of attorney know where to find them. The purpose of this worksheet is for you to record all your digital assets by category, then keep it in a safe place. You will need to share where that 'safe place' is with your solicitor, those with powers of attorney, executor, and other trusted people who would need to have this information. Note that some accounts allow for two-factor authorisation, so a note needs to be made about which accounts those are and how to access the second factor (e.g. app on mobile phone such as Google Authenticator, card in wallet, mobile phone text message code, etc).

The purpose of this form is to capture information related to your digital assets and digital habits. The purpose of this form is not to act as a record of usernames/passwords/PINs.

The answers you provide in this questionnaire will be used to assist your executors in dealing with your estate on your death. These answers will

---

1 Also known as a digital assets inventory worksheet.

also be helpful to your attorney or deputy in the event that you are incapable of dealing with your own affairs.

This worksheet should be kept up to date and reviewed periodically. It is therefore important to date it when you have completed it. This allows for those dealing with your affairs to know that they have the most up-to-date information about your digital assets.

Name ____

Date of preparation/review ______________________________

Do you presently own or make use of computers, smartphone or tablet computing devices? Yes/No

Your electronic devices (e.g. smartphone, tablet, laptop computer, desktop computer)

Name of device	*Identifying features/usual location*	*How to access (PIN, fingerprint recognition, etc)*
Smartphone	Galaxy G4 usually in my handbag	Pin code which my wife knows
Laptop computer	Black Acer laptop which is stored in my home office on the desk	Switch on. There is no password.
...		

Do you use any internet-based data storage services? Yes/No

Do you use any networked, remote or cloud-based storage services? Yes/No

If you answered 'yes' to either of the previous two questions, please complete the details in the following table about the services you use.

Type of storage	WD 2TB Portable Drive
Device's serial number	
Usual location	Home office desk
Types of files stored	Files relating to my eBay sales
Password protection?	
My wishes regarding this device	
Type of storage	Drop box
Device's serial number	n/a
Usual location	Home office desk
Types of files stored	I store and share my family photos here
Password protection?	Yes, it is linked to my Gmail email address
My wishes regarding this device	My children all have access to this Dropbox account. In the event of my death the photographs should be downloaded and copies given to each of my children

Password manager applications (password vault)

Do you presently make use of a secure password management application? Yes/No

Account provider	Dashlane
Account username	…
Account number	
Linked mobile number	…
Linked email	…
Who has access to this application?	My sons Paul and Will
List of sites accessible by this application	

Password authentication applications

Do you presently make use of a secure password authenticator application such as Google Authenticator? Yes/No

Account provider	Google Authenticator
Account username	...
Account number	
Linked mobile number and smartphone	...
Linked email and device	...
Who has access to this application?	My sons Paul and Will
List of sites using this application	HMRC VAT Payments

Financial accounts and mobile payments

Do you presently make use of online banking? Yes/No

If you answered 'yes' to the above, please provide relevant details such as the name of the institutions you do business with online (do not include usernames/passwords/PINs).

I have both business accounts and savings accounts at Santander both of which I access online. I have a NatWest Savings Account and ISA which I access through the app on my phone.

Do you presently use online applications for managing pensions, investments, stocks and shares? Yes/No

Do you presently use online or mobile applications for managing and making mobile payments? Yes/No

If you answered 'yes' to any of the above, please provide relevant details such as the name of the institutions you do business with online. **REMEMBER do not include usernames/passwords/PINs.** These institutions will have their own processes and procedures for closing the accounts of deceased users. They will also have their own procedures to follow in the event you become incapacitated.

Pension company/investment company	Aviva
Investment account website	…
Account number	…
Sort code	…
Password protection?	…
Linked bank accounts	…

Bank account	NatWest
Investment account website	…
Account number	…
Sort code	…
Password protection?	…
Linked accounts	…

Mobile payments account	PayPal
Account website	…
Username	…
Linked email	…
Linked mobile number	…
My wishes	Transfer the balance and close the account

Social media accounts

Do you use any of the following? Or do you have accounts or profiles with them?

Platform	*Yes/No*	*Platform*	*Yes/No*
Twitter		Skype	
Pinterest		Microsoft	
Spotify		Zoom	
Messenger		YouTube	
Snapchat		Facebook inc.	
Instagram		WhatsApp	
TikTok		LinkedIn	

Do you use any of these social media platforms and have an active account? Yes/No

If you answered 'yes' to any of the above, please complete the following table for each platform.

Platform	LinkedIn
Account username/profile	John.Williams
Linked email address	Jwilliams1972@gmail.com
Linked mobile number	...
Linked bank account/credit card	N/A
Memorialise? Legacy contact?	No
My wishes in relation to this account	

Crypto-currency

Do you use any crypto-currency? Yes/No

Do you have any digital wallets type accounts? Yes/No

If you answered 'yes' to any of the above, which platforms do you use?

____

____

____

Please complete the following table for each platform or wallet.

Account provider	Coinbase
Account website	…
Wallet details	…
Linked mobile number	…
Linked email	…
Linked bank account	…

Documents and images (such as PowerPoint presentations, Word and PDF documents, spreadsheets)

Do you store any work files or documents on your personal devices? Yes/No

If you answered 'yes', what documents are they and where are they stored?

____

____

____

Do you store any files or documents on your personal devices which might relate to a charity or voluntary organisation that you are involved with? Yes/No

If you answered 'yes', what documents are they and where are they stored?

____

____

____

Do any of the files or documents stored on your personal devices relate to a business, such as your own business or one in which you work with others, whether in formal partnership or not? Yes/No

If you answered 'yes', what documents are they and where are they stored?

____

____

____

Do you have any system of formally and systematically backing up your electronic documents? Yes/No

If you answered 'yes', how are these backed-up files accessed?

____

____

____

Details of any storage devices or clouds associated with these documents

Type of location	WD 3T External Hard Drive
Protected access method (password/PIN/username/ profile name)	Files access is password protected using the PIN which my wife knows
File details	All my Word, PDF and Office documents are on this drive
Any legal documents/ correspondence? Or documents of a sensitive or delicate nature?	Copies of emails with my solicitor and draft copies of our wills. These are also copied on to my Gmail account
Linked accounts such as a cloud platform providing backups for these files, etc (location of the primary and the backup accounts)	The WD Drive is backed up automatically to the MyCloud account. That backup is linked to my Gmail email address which is registered as the backup email. My mobile phone has the same PIN as the MyCloud Account
Is there a legacy contact/ beneficiary registered with the device/account?	No
My wishes in relation to this account	My wife and my son should be allowed to access the documents and decide what happens to these files
Additional notes in relation to this device/account (Is there data to be removed? Should the files be destroyed or deleted?, etc)	

Ecommerce accounts

Do you buy or sell items online? Yes/No

Do you have any active accounts with online merchants or providers, such as Amazon, eBay, etc? Yes/No

If you answered 'yes' to either of the above, please complete the following table.

Account provider platform	Amazon
Account username/profile	...
Linked bank/payment account	NatWest Current Account Debit Card
Linked mobile number	...
Linked email	...
Who has access?	Linked to my wife's amazon Prime account, through householding tool
Is this a buyer or seller account?	
My wishes	

Gambling and gaming accounts

Account provider	Paddy Power
Account username	...
Account number	
Linked mobile number	...
Linked email	...
Linked bank account	...
My wishes	

A3 An Example of a Letter of Wishes

A letter of wishes is an indication of an individual's wishes, set out in clear, plain English. It is not a legally binding document. It can be prepared by a lay person or a legally qualified individual as circumstances permit.

The format of the example letter of wishes set out below does not need to be applied religiously and can be adapted as needed. Suggested headings are in bold.

Letter of wishes[1]

When used in relation to a last will and testament, the following introductory paragraph should be used:

> I make this letter in reference to my Last Will and Testament dated the [*insert date*] and wish, without imposing any legal obligation on you my Executors and Trustees, that you act on it accordingly.

When used in relation to a trust, including any testamentary trust, the following should be used:

> I make this letter in reference to my Trust dated the [*insert date*] which confers discretionary powers on you as my Trustees. I appreciate that I cannot fetter your discretion or determine the way in which you exercise your powers. In the hope that this may be of help to you in exercising your discretionary powers, but without imposing any binding legal or equitable obligations on you or seeking to prevent you from acting as you think best in light of changing circumstances, I would ask you to have regard to my wishes expressed below.

---

1 Also known as a memorandum of wishes when used in relation to a testamentary trust.

> The matters in this letter should also be read in reference to the Digital Assets Inventory, copies of which can be found [*insert location*]

(Include the above clause if a digital assets inventory is being used. Ideally, two copies of both this letter and the digital assets inventory should be kept in two distinctly separate places to protect from fire, flood, theft or act of God.)

Social media

> It is my wish that my account/accounts with [*insert platform name*] (*delete as necessary*) are deleted/memorialised (*as appropriate*)

Examples:

> It is my wish that my account with Facebook is memorialised. I have named Jane Smith as my legacy contact to undertake this work.
>
> It is my wish that my accounts with Instagram are deleted, and I request that you take care of this matter. The profile name and login information is stored in my smartphone app.
>
> It is my wish that my account with LinkedIn is memorialised and placed into Remembrance mode. I request that you take care of this matter.

Email accounts

> I am the registered user of [*insert address*] and [*insert email address*] (*delete as necessary*) and you can find them saved on my [*insert*] (*device, i.e. stable*)

In the event that the login information (or linked to a password manager application) is required, a note of it can be made here. This is not required if the client is completing and/or maintaining the digital asset inventory.

Hardware/devices

It should be remembered that certain individuals may be given particular items, as in a traditional letter of wishes:

> While I have not named a beneficiary or legacy to inherit my [*insert*] (*e.g. computers, smartphone, tablets, etc*), I wish them to go to [*insert*] (*e.g. my wife*). I would however like all the family photos on those devices to be copied and provided to [*insert*] (*e.g. my brother and sister*).

Example:

> I would like my Grandson, James Smith to be given my collection of Sega games, including my Sonic the Hedgehog paraphernalia.

(The clause above is a good example of a disposition that may have a particularly sentimental meaning as opposed to a financial one.)

Website login/passwords

It should be remembered that if website login details and/or passwords are accounted for in the digital assets inventory, they do not have to be set out in a letter of wishes. Where there is no such digital assets inventory, they can be set out in the following format.

Website address	
Username/login/password	
Associated email address	

The letter of wishes approach may be appropriate where there is a limited number of such items to list. If a more numerous list is required, the inventory approach is recommended.

Bills paid/accessed online

The letter of wishes can also simplify matters, such as helping personal representatives and/or executors to locate electronic copies of documents:

- Council tax or utility bill payments:

1 Bill type (e.g. *council tax payment*)

Registered email address	
Website address	
Username/login/password	
Payment type (e.g. monthly, quarterly, annually)	

2 Bill type (e.g. *gas bill payment*)

Registered email address	
Website address	
Username/login/password	
Payment type (e.g. monthly, quarterly, annually)	

- Credit hire statements, stockbroker portfolios or pension documents:

1 Account number and provider information (e.g. *pension provider*)

Registered email address	
Website address	
Username/login/password	
Payment type (e.g. monthly, quarterly, annually)	

2 Account number and provider information (*e.g. car hire payments*)

Registered email address Website address Username/login/password Payment type (e.g. monthly, quarterly, annually)	

This information can then be used to contact the provider to suspend the online account access and deal with the accounts in the probate process.

Signature and date

The letter of wishes does not need to be witnessed but should be signed and dated by the testator. Ideally, pages should also be numbered, and two copies of each completed document should be made.

Index

References are to page numbers.